NATALIE WILLMAN DUFFY is professor and coordinator of dance at Fairleigh Dickinson University, Teaneck, New Jersey. She initiated and developed the Dance Concentration at FDU and has directed the Dance Group for several years. Professor Duffy has also published articles on dance and physical education.

D1510218

Natalie Willman Duffy

MODERN DANCE
AN ADULT BEGINNER'S GUIDE

A SPECTRUM BOOK

PRENTICE-HALL, INC.   Englewood Cliffs, New Jersey 07632

Library of Congress Cataloging in Publication Data

Duffy, Natalie.
  Modern dance.

  "A Spectrum Book."
  Bibliography: p.
  Includes Index.
  1. Modern dance. I. Title.
GV1783.D73 1982   793.3'2   82-7706
ISBN 0-13-590935-X   AACR2
ISBN 0-13-590927-9 (pbk.)

A SPECTRUM BOOK

10 9 8 7 6 5 4 3 2 1

Printed in the United States of America

ISBN 0-13-590927-9 {PBK.}

ISBN 0-13-590935-X

Editorial/production supervision and interior design by Cyndy Lyle Rymer
Manufacturing buyer Cathie Lenard
Cover design by April Blair Stewart
Frontispiece photo by Marj Cox

Prentice-Hall International, Inc., *London*
Prentice-Hall of Australia Pty. Limited, *Sydney*
Prentice-Hall Canada Inc., *Toronto*
Prentice-Hall of India Private Limited, *New Delhi*
Prentice-Hall of Japan, Inc., *Tokyo*
Prentice-Hall of Southeast Asia Pte. Ltd., *Singapore*
Whitehall Books Limited, *Wellington, New Zealand*
Editora Prentice-Hall do Brasil LTDA., Rio de Janeiro

CONTENTS

PREFACE

Modern Dance introduces you to the world of dance, not as a spectator, critic, or historian, but kinesthetically as a participant.

Why is a textbook necessary? Everyone knows that one does not learn to dance in the library but only by dancing! Every human endeavor in art or science requires a structured body of knowledge as an adjunct to other learning experiences. This book can be used for self-study or in conjunction with a course in modern dance. Although creative movement experiences are intensely personal and there is no possibility of "right or wrong" in the solution of movement problems, you will benefit immensely from the stimulation of a teacher and classmates. It is important to find a knowledgeable teacher and a sympathetic class and then to "jump right in" to the first class. The materials for classes in modern dance are outlined in this book. With an understanding of these basic concepts, a student or an instructor can formulate his or her own class.

Typically, a class includes a warm-up, sometimes conducted by the teacher but often done by each dancer on his or her own; group experiences in techniques taught by the teacher; movement through space—locomotor movements done from one end of the studio to the other; and opportunities for creative movement. But after participating in an hour's activity, it is not always easy to remember what has been done, and this text will serve as a review. Or, if you are enrolled in a dance course for academic credit, this book can be used as a refresher before examinations.

The material is intended for adults who are beginners in modern dance. Most have elected to study dance purely for pleasure and have no professional aspirations. Their choice of modern dance is a wise one, for it is a dance form which utilizes natural movements. Many mature students have been programmed to move in certain ways, but this book encourages them to overcome their inhibitions and unleash their freedom to move. Students who aspire to professional careers in dance will also find use for this text. Their early training is the same, although they proceed to more complex techniques. Also, some professional dancers become highly skilled technicians without a clear understanding of the theory of dance for which their technique is needed. This book presents some of this basic information.

Many "schools" of modern dance have developed, resulting in the various styles of movement that characterize their leaders. An attempt is made here not to explain these styles but to present material that enables the reader to understand the underlying concepts of movement and how dance develops from these.

The emphasis of this text is not on the preparation of highly skilled technicians but rather on the presentation of concepts and suggestions for creative activity. Of course one should always try to improve one's technique, but one should also strive to grow creatively and intellectually by exploring movement, watching performances live and on film, and reading about dance. Dance study is not merely gymnastic training but an introduction to humanity's oldest art form. Even if you do not intend to continue the technical study of dance beyond one semester, a brief experience can make you a part of a more appreciative dance audience for the rest of your life.

The techniques in Chapter 2 have been developed during many years of teaching modern dance classes. Some can be traced to study at the Boston-Bouvé School, where the late Pauline Chellis introduced me to modern dance. Others originated from professional study at the Martha Graham School of Contemporary Dance and other schools. There is also perhaps a trace of influence from the study of gymnastics and yoga. As you become an experienced dancer, you will continue to learn and evolve variations of techniques for preparing the body for dance. You will eventually develop a *barre* of your own that is comfortable for you.[1] Older dancers will find that the time required for warming up is somewhat longer. The exercises presented here are simple ones to help you prepare your instrument for artistic expression.

Chapters 3 and 4 introduce the elements of dance and specific ways to explore movement possibilities. These suggestions are offered in the hope that they will increase your understanding of the elements of movement and will help to prepare you for the craft of choreography, which is discussed in Chapter 5. Chapter 6 is intended for those students who elect to perform the compositions of others or to present original works. Those who are charged with responsibility for the production of a performance will also find practical suggestions.

Dance is a creative activity. You will find that the more you study and practice, the more easily you will discover your creative talents.

ACKNOWLEDGMENTS

I wish to acknowledge the inspiration and training received from Pauline Chellis, Martha Graham, Louis Horst, Barbara Nash, and Lucille Verhulst.

The countless modern dance students at Fairleigh Dickinson University who, over the years, experimented with the materials presented here are also to be thanked.

---

[1] In this case, *barre* means a series of warm-up exercises that become a routine part of each day's practice.

The section on performance is dedicated to past and present members of the Fairleigh Dickinson University Dance Group who have been "through it all" with me!

Special appreciation is due to the dancers who modeled for the photographic illustrations: Alena Arent, Colleen Ball, Fred Bailey, Kimberly Baynes, Lynn Boucher, Christan Francisco, Rosellen Ivory, Barbara Kingston, Linda Lehovec, Kathleen Lucas, Dina McDermott, and Stephanie Paul. The photography was done by Fairleigh Dickinson University photographers, especially Marj Cox. Merry McCrimlisk, Director of University Relations, helped make it possible.

The figure drawings were created by E. Scott Lucia, and the diagrams by Henry Duffy.

I also wish to thank Mary Kennan, Editor, Spectrum Books, for her friendly cooperation.

1

WHAT IS
MODERN DANCE?

The dance is the mother of the arts.
Music and poetry exist in time;
painting and architecture in space.
But the dance lives at once in time and space.
The creator and the thing created,
the artist and the work are still
one and the same thing.[1]

Modern dance is often concerned with the communication of emotions or ideas through the medium of movement; sometimes it is concerned simply with movement itself. Modern dance developed in the early part of the twentieth century as a revolt against the stylized formality of ballet. Each of its earliest exponents searched for ways of utilizing natural movement as a means of artistic expression suitable to the times.

The term *modern dance* has often been a confusing one. Some people think of current popular social dances as modern dance. There is, in addition, another more serious confusion. Because the development of modern dance paralleled the development of "modern" music and "modern" art, the name, at the time, seemed applicable. But, because modern dance is a contemporary art form and is an expression of the individuals who practice it, it is constantly changing, and the term *contemporary dance* may be more appropriate.

The instrument of dance is the body, and as John Martin said, the dancer "...not only needs to know how to play his instrument, but he must build it out of himself

[1]Curt Sachs, *World History of the Dance* (New York:W.W. Norton & Co., Inc., 1937), p. 3.

FIGURE 1-1
Modern dance draws
its materials from natural
human movement.
Peter Krayer

and keep it tuned at all times."[2] Herein lies the difference between dance and the other arts, and also one difference between modern dance and other dance styles.

Modern dance has no established steps or patterns; the dancer must create his or her own emanating from movements of the body. In time, different styles of movement have emerged from the techniques of its leading exponents. Those stylistic differences have created a vocabulary of movement drawn from natural human movement. The uniqueness of modern dance is the freedom of each dancer to build his or her own movements; to go beyond what has previously been done.

How did modern dance come about? Since earliest times, essentially all peoples of the world have danced. Anthropologists and dance historians have surmised that early man may have learned to dance from watching birds and animals as they performed courting rituals and other dance-like movements. Evidence about early dance comes from rock and cave paintings, and from the dances of primitive societies that are still in existence. There is reason to believe that dance was one of early man's greatest preoccupations. It was a vehicle for religious

[2]John Martin, "Isadora Duncan and Basic Dance," in *Isadora Duncan*, Paul Magriel, ed. (New York: Henry Holt & Co., Inc., 1947), p. 12.

expression, used to appease the spirits or to make specific requests. Religion remained a major reason for dance until the Middle Ages.

Dance was also a common means of social communication and part of the celebration of major events such as birth, coming of age, marriage, death, harvest, and the return of victorious warriors or hunters. Children were taught the history and mores of the tribe through dance.

In addition, dance was used therapeutically, to heal the sick or to drive away the evil spirits causing distress.

Because of primitive man's great awe of the forces of nature and of animals, his dance was often imitative of animals or of the spirits he worshipped. Early dancers wore skins, feathers and tails, painted their faces, or donned masks. Their posture was often crouched with stamping of bare feet and clenched fists. Their movements, although simple, sometimes became intensely frenzied and required great endurance. Some dances resulted in a hypnotic state of the participants. Men were the major dancers, and women often accompanied them with chants or clapping. When women also danced, the sexes were usually segregated. At first the circle was the most common dance pattern. Later the serpentine formation with a leader was used, and eventually a line of dancers or two parallel lines were utilized. Accompaniment for dance consisted of body sounds made with the voice or with the clapping of hands or stamping of feet. Gourds, rattles, bells, and drums added to the variety of sounds. At first, everyone danced. Later dance leaders were selected—the shaman, medicine man, or witch doctor.

As civilization advanced, dance was divided into two avenues: the communal which we now refer to as folk dance, and the theatrical which requires trained dancers as performers.

In ancient Egypt, dance remained an integral part of the educational process, the celebration of religious rituals and social events, and as an important aspect of the funeral rites and the preparation for life after death. The gods now resembled humans more closely and the kings were considered divine.

Written evidence of dance as well as depictions in paintings and art objects have been uncovered. In most of these one sees dancers and musicians together. The harp, flute, drum, lute, castanets, and voice are among the many accompaniments for dance.

The development of the professional dancer continued with slaves and later with "free men" who entertained with their acrobatic feats. Dance became less spontaneous as a vocabulary of steps and movements developed.

The role of dance in ancient Greece reached an apex in education and religious expression and became a significant companion to the development of drama. Mythology relates many tales of dance. We hear of rousing war dances, of fertility dances which involve acrobatic stunts, of women's skirt dances, and funeral dances. There were great festivals at the temple, many to honor Dionysius. We are told of a dance mania in which women danced the *oreibasia*, a frenzied dance characterized by screaming and dashing through the woods on cold winter nights with flowing gowns and streaming hair, carrying drums and flaming torches of pine cones, while tearing snakes to bits. These women became known as maenads or baccantes.[3] The men sang and danced and drank wine to honor Dionysius. Their costumes of goat skins, tails, hoofs, and head pieces gave them the name satyr or goatman. One of their dances was called the *dithyramb*.

Festivals, ceremonies, and athletic events included dance, the chorus, and drama. From the writings of Sophocles, Euripides, Socrates, Plato, and Aristotle one realizes the importance of dance at this time in history. It is the study of these works and the ancient greek statues that is said to have inspired Isadora Duncan and other later dancers.

The medieval days have been referred to as the Dark Days of Dance because of the Christian religion's disapproval of dance. Although there was little development of theatrical dance during that time, some religious dance remained and folk dance flourished. This was the period of the dance of death described in art, music, and literature, and of the dancing manias that occurred throughout Europe.

During the late Middle Ages and the Renaissance,

[3]Lillian B. Lawler, *The Dance in Ancient Greece* (Middletown, CT: Weslyan University Press, 1964), p. 74-75.

ballet became an entertainr ent for the elite. The Ballet Comique de la Reine commissioned by Catherine de Medici and choreographed by Balthasar de Beaujoyeux in 1581 is credited as being the first major "ballet." It lasted five hours and included elaborate sets, music, drama, mythology, and the nobility as actors and dancers. Ballet continued to develop in Europe, especially during the reign of Louis XIV who was himself a dancer. Because of the nobility's involvement in the performance of ballet and also in the balls that followed, the ballet master became important. Early dance manuals show that the dance master taught courtly manners as well as the latest steps. At this time music was written for the dance. What we now call classical ballet was in its earliest stages.

Ballet continued to develop in Europe and Russia. During the early 1800s romantic ballet reached a pinnacle. But, by the late nineteenth century, its fire was dwindling and in America most ballet was either imported or imitative. No wonder that this growing country was ready to embrace a new dance form.

In the United States in the beginning of the twentieth century, Isadora Duncan rebelled against the formality and structure of ballet, and her experiments in free movement gave birth to what we now call modern or contemporary dance. Duncan had essentially no formal training in dance and she states that she was born near the sea and that her first knowledge of movement came from "the rhythm of the waves."[4] Later she stood motionless for hours searching for the core of movement which she claimed to be the solar plexus. "I spent long days and nights in the studio seeking that dance which might be the divine expression of the human spirit through the medium of the body's movement."[5] Those who saw Isadora Duncan dance were impressed by the sincerity and emotional expression of this untrained dancer and free spirit. Her art and her life were ahead of her time. Was she the founder of modern dance? Isadora Duncan certainly did not develop the dance of today, but her major contribution was her independent spirit manifested through her dance. Her

[4]Isadora Duncan, *My Life* (New York: Boni and Liveright, 1927), p. 10.
[5]*Ibid*, p. 75.

FIGURE 1-2
Isadora Duncan
Dance Collection, The New York Public
Library at Lincoln Center.
Used with permission.

FIGURE 1-3
Ruth St. Denis and Ted Shawn.
Dance Collection, The New York Public
Library at Lincoln Center.
Used with permission.

successors perpetuated her spirit of independence rather
than preserving her technique of dance.

Ruth St. Denis and Ted Shawn, artists, performers,
and educators, pioneered in dance as an art form. Ruth St.
Denis's delight was exotic dances of the Far East and Asia.
Her husband's work with the Denishawn Company and
School complimented Ruth St. Denis's talent and dedica-
tion. The Denishawn School taught technique of many
different styles of dance, both American and ethnic. The
company toured the world and developed modern dance
as a theatrical art form. Later, after their separation,
Shawn's work with Springfield College physical education
students (all males in those days) helped Americans to see
that dance could be strong and manly. From the careful
training of the Denishawn School emerged the next generation of rebels: Martha Graham, Doris Humphrey, and
Charles Weidman. These three, although successful performers and teachers at Denishawn, did not feel that the
philosophies of St. Denis and Shawn answered their needs
to develop their own dance form which would be an

appropriate expression of their individual contemporary ideas about movement.

When Graham went to the Eastman School of Music to teach in 1925, she began her own experiments in dance. With some of her students from Eastman she presented her first concert in New York City in 1926. Musician Louis Horst, who had also abandoned Denishawn, was her accompanist. He later became her musical director and eventually taught choreography to dancers on the basis of his knowledge of musical forms. Martha Graham nurtured modern dance as theatre dance. Her technique of movement was at first simple and stark, and her themes deep and mysterious. Many of her earlier audiences were puzzled. Graham's productivity was enormous, and her creations have numbered about two hundred dances. *Primitive Mysteries*, with music by Louis Horst; *Appalachian Spring*, with music by Aaron Copland; *Clytemnestra*, music by Halim El-Dabh; *Seraphic Dialogue*, music by Norman Dello Joio, are only a few. Graham developed as a concert dancer of unusual virtuosity and as a superb choreographer, and as her company of three young Eastman girls expanded she formed a school of dance and developed a technique of movement based on breath rhythms. Anyone who has taken classes at the Martha

FIGURE 1-5
Doris Humphrey
and Charles Weidman
Dance Collection,
The New York Public
Library at Lincoln Center,
Astor, Lenox
and Tilden Foundations.
Used with permission.

Graham School of Contemporary Dance knows the rigors of learning the contractions and releases which are central to the Graham style of movement. Her technique originates from the center of the body and follows a natural sequence of contraction and release that is indigenous to all muscles whenever movement occurs.

After leaving Denishawn, Doris Humphrey and Charles Weidman formed a company and a school. Doris Humphrey's technique of movement remained more lyrical and softer than that of Graham. Her technique was also the result of observations of natural human movement. She began her search for answers by standing still before a mirror. In this position there was a tendency for the body to fall and her muscles responded in order to counteract gravity. "Dance, then," she ascertained, "lay in the arc between two deaths, the lassitude of the body erect and of the body prone."[6] In addition to the fall and recovery, Humphrey's technique encompassed the use of breath rhythms, oppositional motion, changes of weight, and successional flow.[7] Humphrey's training of students was

[6]Selma Jeanne Cohen, (an autobiography edited and completed) *Doris Humphrey: An Artist First.* (Middletown, CT: Wesleyan University Press, 1972), p. 119.

[7]For further insight into Doris Humphrey's technique, the reader is referred to Ernestine Stodelle, *The Dance Technique of Doris Humphrey: and Its Creative Potential* (Princeton, NJ: Princeton Book Company, Pub., 1978).

unique in that hers was a twofold approach: technique and the encouragment of creativity.

The Humphrey-Weidman Company began to present concerts in New York in 1928 and to tour in 1935. Humphrey's contribution was most notable in the area of composition. A few of her many beautifully choreographed dances are *Air for the G String* and *Passacaglia in C Minor*, with music by Bach, *The Shakers*, accompaniment by Pauline Lawrence, *New Dance* and *With My Red Fires* set to scores by Riegger, and *Dionysiaques*, music by Schmitt. Humphrey was more concerned with group choreography than with the soloist.

Later when illness prematurely ended Humphrey's performing career she continued to choreograph for José Limon and his company, and for the Julliard Dance Theatre. An articulate writer, Humphrey's concise rules for choreography found in *The Art of Making Dances*,[8] are invaluable for students of dance.

Much of Charles Weidman's choreography was concerned with American themes: *A House Divided* and *Lynch Town*, for example. His unique contribution was his use of humor and pantomime in modern dance. *And Daddy Was a Fireman*, *Flickers*, and *Fables Of Our Time* are notable examples.

At the same period of time a similar movement was underway in Germany, spearheaded by Mary Wigman, a disciple of Emile Jaques-Dalcrose and Rudolf von Laban.[9] Wigman sought to find a new language of movement to express emotion. At first her technique was developed without music, only body rhythms. Later she utilized percussive accompaniment. Wigman's experiments in movement led to what she termed "absolute dance" and resulted in a system of movement based on tension and relaxation. It is interesting to note the similarity to Graham's contraction and release, although the two artists developed these theories on different continents, apparently uninfluenced by each other. Both arrived at their conclusions after closely observing muscular action. In

[8]Doris Humphrey, *The Art of Making Dances*. ed. Barbara Pollack (New York: Rinehart & Company, Inc., 1959).

[9]Emile Jaques-Dalcrose (1865–1950) developed *eurythmics*, a system of rhythmic study through the use of movement. Rudolf von Laban (1879–1958) developed effort/shape movement analysis, and a system of notating movement which formed the basis for Labanotation.

1931, after her concert tour of the United States, Sol Hurok suggested that Wigman open a school of dance in New York. Her pupil, Hanya Holm, was chosen to bring the Wigman style of movement to America.

While teaching the Wigman concepts to American modern dancers, Holm was adjusting to her adopted country and formulating her own philosophy of dance. In 1936, it became necessary for political reasons to change the name of the school to the Hanya Holm School of Dance. In her unique approach to teaching technique, theory and composition seemed to be inseparable and her students were offered experiences in improvisation. She choreographed and performed with a concert group, but one of her major contributions was her development of the lecture-demonstration. Through this she helped to acquaint colleges throughout the country with this new dance form called modern dance.

Along with Graham, Humphrey, and Weidman, Holm taught at the Bennington Summer School of the Dance and it was there that her most acclaimed work, *Trend*, with music by Wallingford Riegger and Edgard Varése, was premiered in 1937.

Holm choreographed musicals for Broadway such as *Kiss Me Kate* and *My Fair Lady*, and also for opera, plays, movies, and television.

The next generation of American dance innovators studied with, or were influenced by, Graham, Humphrey, Weidman, or Holm. They also reached beyond the teachings of their mentors and added to the scope of movement experience. José Limon, Merce Cunningham, Erick Hawkins, Paul Taylor, and Alwin Nikolais are notable examples of this group.

Agnes de Mille's "modern" ballet choreography helped to bridge the gap between classical ballet and modern dance. Her choreography for Broadway musicals set a precedent that has been followed by other choreographers from both the ballet and modern dance disciplines. Among de Mille's many successes are *Oklahoma!, Carousel, Brigadoon*, and *Gentlemen Prefer Blondes*.

By the mid-twentieth century, modern dance had become a unique American dance style, firmly established on the concert stage and taught in colleges and universities. The work of Margaret H'Doubler at the University of

FIGURE 1-6
José Limon
Dance Collection, The
New York Public Library
at Lincoln Center.
Used with permission.

FIGURE 1-7
Erick Hawkins as "First Man" in *Plains Daybreak*
Photo by Peter Papadopolous

FIGURE 1-8
Agnes de Mille
Photo by Jack Mitchell

Wisconsin, and Martha Hill at Bennington College Summer School of Dance, gave physical education and dance teachers the understanding and materials necessary to teach modern dance. Modern dance was the first theatre form of dance to invade the schools; ballet and jazz dance followed. The advent of movement education in the elementary schools gave children the foundation for later study of dance.[10] In the 1960s and 1970s another group of innovators explored dance in different ways; they called it pure dance, new dance, experimental dance, minimal dance, post-modern dance, or non-literal dance. Avant garde choreographers even used nondancers, or no movement, or no sound, or no stage, and so on. There was often no attempt to express emotions or to tell a story. As has usually been the case throughout history, the development of dance closely reflects the development in art and music. For example, performance pieces and "happenings" in art have similarities to the work of these choreographers. Robert Rauschemberg, Jasper Johns, and Andy Warhol are some of the painters who collaborated with Merce Cunningham, Paul Taylor and other choreographers.

The names Twyla Tharp, Anna Halprin, Yvonne Rainer, Meredith Monk, Don Redlich, Trisha Brown, Laura Dean, and the Pilobolus Dance Theater are among many of this group of innovators. Some, such as Twyla Tharp, expanded the scope of modern dance by choreographing for ballet companies, ice skaters, and Broadway musicals as well as for modern dance groups.

In the 1980s there is more interest than ever in dance as a theatre art. There are groups that perform classical ballet, jazz dance, and ethnic dance as well as modern dance. Some, such as Alvin Ailey Dance Theatre and the Joffrey Ballet, perform works from more than one style of dance. Other groups present multimedia or "total theatre" performances. To become a successful professional dancer, one must be trained in the major styles of dance. Television can be credited with offering to a larger number of people than ever before the opportunity to view a variety of excellent dance groups. Major dance companies based

[10]Movement education teaches children to be aware of their own potential for effective movement and of how to use these movement skills in daily activities and in sports, as well as how to use their bodies creatively as instruments of communication.

FIGURE 1-9
Twyla Tharp in "Eight
Jelly Rolls" (1974)
Photo by Tony Russell

FIGURE 1-10
Don Redlich
Photo by John Lindquist

in large cities tour the world, and regional companies perform in smaller cities.

The recent increased awareness of the benefits of physical activity to one's sense of well-being has resulted in the tremendous popularity of active rather than spectator roles. Participation in jogging and sports such as tennis and racquetball seem to be at an all-time high. As Martha Graham has said, dancers are "divine athletes."[11] Despite major differences between professional and popular dance, this perhaps explains why so many people are studying one of the various dance forms today and enjoying recreational dance such as disco.

Because the material of dance is movement, and the body is the instrument, it is necessary to study movement in space, time, and force. The chapters which follow will help you to understand these essential elements and how they are utilized in the craft of choreography. The fourth component of dance is of course, the body as the instrument. To be eloquent in expressing the vocabulary of dance, the instrument must be educated, trained, and constantly kept in condition. To begin that training, various systems of dance techniques have evolved. The next chapters introduce you to some simple exercises and to the world of exploration in movement.

[11]Walter Terry, *Frontiers of Dance* (New York: Thomas Y. Crowell Company, Inc., 1975), p. 136.

2

GETTING STARTED: TECHNIQUES

Don your leotard, find your "space," and let's begin! Modern dance has no prescribed steps, positions, or patterns. Beginning students are often puzzled. How, then, does one learn to dance? One learns by training the body to be an articulate instrument for expression through movement. The range of movement of which the body is capable must be expanded, refined, polished. The body must be made strong, flexible, and controlled. Do not be misled by the often heard misconception that modern dance gives one the opportunity to do "one's own thing" and that there is therefore no need for discipline or technique. It is through a disciplined body that the dancer is able to speak with clarity and conviction. This is achieved by hours of technical study over the course of many years. The tools for this training are often referred to as warm-up exercises, dance techniques, and movement patterns. Martha Graham has said that it takes ten years to make a dancer.[1] Do not despair; perhaps you will not appear on the concert stage immediately, but you can enjoy the sense of freedom of movement and kinesthetic accomplishment in your first dance class. If you approach each class as if it were a performance, you will find that your proficiency will accelerate.

Modern dance is a personal form of dance. Do not compare yourself to others; be concerned only with your own progress. How you feel during class will tell you much, mirrors will help you to see how you look, and your teacher will give you helpful criticisms. Differences in

[1]Walter Terry, *Frontiers of Dance: The Life of Martha Graham* (New York: Thomas Y. Crowell Company, Inc., 1975), p. 57.

FIGURE 2-1
Preparation for dance
Peter Krayer

body types influence one's way of moving. Previous training in dance, sports, and gymnastics have accustomed
your body to movement experiences. Then, too, you will
discover that people have inherent movement preferences:
some move quickly and sharply, others flow through life.
These individual movement differences reflect both per-
sonality and physiology and can enhance the class experience. Do not view the diversity in a competitive manner,
but develop your own style of movement and profit from
exposure to the movements of others. For success on the
concert stage, technical excellence is essential. To understand, appreciate, and enjoy dance, such a degree of
proficiency is not necessary, but continual improvement of
technique will enhance your enjoyment. In addition, be
mindful that an instrument of communication must have
something worthwhile to say. Each of us has the potential
for creativity if we allow ourselves to utilize it.

If your movement background is in gymnastics, cal-
isthenics, yoga, or ballet, you will notice some similarities
in spite of the uniqueness of the modern dance training.
The pioneers who are responsible for the development of
modern dance were searching for natural movement of the
human body. Some, such as Isadora Duncan and Ruth St.
Denis, were influenced by Delsarte techniques.[2] Some of
the innovators were relatively untrained in established
dance forms, and therefore their discoveries were truly
unique ways of moving. As you experience and practice

[2]The Delsarte method of expressive action was developed by François
Delsarte in nineteenth-century France. The system is based on the use of gesture
as a means of communication.

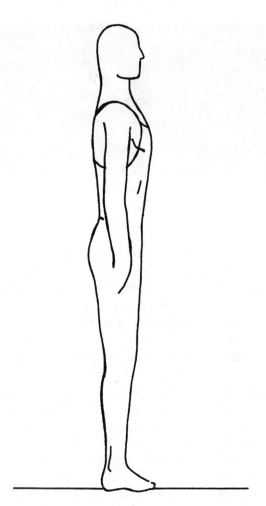

FIGURE 2-2
Proper alignment
E. Scott Lucia

various techniques of modern dance, your body will become freer and in time you will develop your own movement patterns and will begin to experience the art of dance.

Before beginning to dance, a word must be said about body alignment. Proper alignment means that when standing, sitting, or moving, the various parts of the body should be so arranged that there is a minimum of stress on any part.

Stand before a mirror or with a friend to check each area. Stand with feet parallel and just an inch or two apart. Your weight should be supported by the toes, balls of the feet, heels, and outer edges of the feet. The arches should not be touching the floor. If you ever walked on a cement floor with wet feet you probably saw footprints like the ones in the diagram. If, however, your feet are pronated and arches are close to or touching the floor, the situation can be improved by rotating the knees outward. The knees should be directly over the ankles and in line with the center of the hips. The knees should be straight but not hyperextended. A side view in the mirror will help you do this. Continuing upward, are the shoulders lined up over the hips and the ear lobes directly over the shoulders? If you discover a swayback or lordosis, rotate the hips under a bit. Imagine having a dinosaur tail that pulls your hips downward. There are, of course, inherited differences in the amount of curvature of the spine, but one should not allow the situation to be exaggerated. The abdomen should be pulled in and the chest slightly lifted. The shoulders should be pulled back, but not enough to create the appearance of a toy soldier; the shoulders should be relaxed and dropped. Arms hang in a relaxed manner at the sides. A side view peek in the mirror will detect a head which is too far forward.

Now face the mirror to determine whether one shoulder or hip is higher than the other. This could mean scoliosis (deviation of the spine) or just a bad habit pattern from carrying books or a briefcase too frequently on one side.

Correct posture is worth developing. Not only does it enhance one's appearance, but it will also help you to prevent injuries, avoid fatigue, low back pain, and other ailments resulting from stress due to improper alignment. When correct body alignment becomes habitual, you will utilize proper body mechanics when in motion, whether it be dance, sports, lifting weights, or just everyday activities of studying, catching buses, and carrying suitcases. Although frequently difficult, postural correction can become habitual, as evidenced by the carriage of West Point graduates which becomes permanent.

In technique class, rhythmic accompaniment is important in order to respond to externally imposed rhythm. Teachers often use a piano accompanist, record player, tape recorder, percussion instrument, or their own voices. Alwin Nikolais has led the way in his ingenious use of

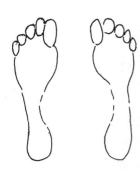

FIGURE 2-3
Weight-bearing portions
of the feet
Henry Duffy

FIGURE 2-4
Alwin Nikolais (1974)
Bruce Pomerantz

percussion instruments. Dancers can also explore the possibilities of moving to internal body rhythms: one's pulse or breath rhythm.

Rhythmic accompaniment is even more important when a class or a group attempts to move in unison. The discipline learned from orderly rows of bending and stretching bodies in concert is helpful in preparing the dancer for ensemble dancing. Some dancers seem to inherit more responsiveness to musical accompaniment than others, but musicality can be enhanced, and the foundations for this training begin in the technique class.

For clarity, the following dance techniques and exercises are grouped according to starting position. You will obviously not want to do all the exercises from any one group but rather choose one or more from each category for your class or practice session. It is wise to start with exercises which do not require balance and then progress to those demanding greater coordination, speed, and energy. You may want to return to the simpler ones for a brief period of relaxation or "cooling down" as the class terminates.

It is advisable to start class sitting or lying on the floor because at the beginning of a class it is easier to concentrate on movement without the encumbrance of the force of gravity. As the muscles become warm, the dancer graduates from sitting or lying on the floor to kneeling or half-kneeling, then to standing, and finally to moving through space, which is called locomotor movement. The techniques are not specific to any "school" of modern dance, although those which involve contractions and releases must be credited to the influence of Martha Graham.

TECHNIQUES

There are two bent-knee sitting positions frequently used. Sit with legs crossed, as tailors sit.

Bent-Knee Sitting Positions

Sit with the soles of the feet together; this is sometimes called frog sitting.

In either arrangement of the feet and legs, the knees fall outward to a position as close to the floor as the flexibility of the hip extensors (sartorii) will allow. The back is

FIGURE 2-5
Tailor sitting position
E. Scott Lucia

FIGURE 2-6
Frog sitting position
E. Scott Lucia

straight, and the hands are resting on the ankles or on the floor at the sides or are held in first position. In first position the arms are raised forward to chest height in a curved position with hands pointing inward.

| STRETCHES

Sitting with the soles of the feet together and the hands on the ankles, rock gently from side to side. You will discover two "sitting bones" (tuberosities of the ischia). It is important to be familiar with these two bony protuberances, for you will be using them when sitting in several positions. Now, gently relax your turned-out knees toward the floor several times. This will help to increase flexibility and prepare your "turnout."

Remain in the same sitting position, hands on ankles, and gently lean forward from the hips, keeping the back straight. Stretch forward a given number of times. Alternate these movements with the same number of gentle stretches with a rounded back, bringing the head toward the floor. It is not necessary to return to upright sitting after each forward movement; instead, stay comfortably stretched and then stretch a bit farther each time.[3]

[3]In the past, the terms bounce or bob were used to describe these stretches, but when ballistic bouncing is improperly performed, it can be dangerous. It is therefore preferable to think in terms of relax and stretch.

Head, neck, and shoulder exercises are easily done in nearly any position: tailor sitting, frog sitting, kneeling, standing, or even while sitting at your desk. It is important that the back remain straight and that there be no movement of any other part of the body, for these are "isolation" exercises.

HEAD AND NECK Drop the head forward until the chin rests on the chest. Lift the head to upright position. Drop the head backward. Return. Drop the head to the side, ear toward the shoulder. (Do not bring the shoulder toward the ear.) Return. Repeat to the other side. Turn the head to the side as if to look abruptly to the right. Return to center. Repeat to the other side. Now make slow circles with the head by allowing the weight of the head to carry it downward, to the side, backward, sideward, and forward. Make two circles in one direction and then repeat to the other side.

SHOULDERS When shoulder exercises are done, the arms should hang limply and follow along naturally. Lift one shoulder as high as possible, then drop. Repeat with the other shoulder. Lift both shoulders simultaneously. Drop. Push one shoulder forward, return to center, push backward, return to center. Repeat with the other shoulder. Repeat with both shoulders. Rotate one shoulder forward. Rotate the shoulder backward. Repeat with the other shoulder. Repeat with both shoulders simultaneously or in opposition.

3. LEG TURNOUT

In frog sitting position, lift the arms in front of the chest in a slightly rounded position. Keeping the joint at the base of the little toes in contact with the floor and the legs turned out from the hips, slide the legs forward. Press forward with the heels so that the feet are becoming flexed. The heels are off the floor, however, and the turnout occurs from the hips, so the whole leg is rotated outward. When the legs are fully extended, extend the abducted (turned-out) feet, flex them again, and return the legs to the starting position in the same manner. As the plié (bend) occurs, the heels are off the floor. Arms remain in front of the chest throughout, and the back and head are held erect.

4. CONTRACTION AND RELEASE[4]

Sit in tailor or frog position, arms at shoulder height, slightly rounded toward the front, palms facing downward. Contract the abdominal muscles. You will discover that the back will round as a result, and the shoulders will move forward slightly. The rounded shoulders should be directly over the hips, which are slightly tilted backward. The arms remain at shoulder height but rotate so that the palms and forearms are now supine. The palms are cupped. The important thing to remember is that the neck muscles are not involved and therefore must not be allowed to become tense. Before the release, the body is flexed at the hips. Release the muscles of the abdomen; as a result the back will straighten over the floor and the head, arms, and trunk return to starting position. The release is a strong movement. It must not be thought of simply as a relaxation.

FIGURE 2-7
Contraction in frog sitting position
Ken Roesser

[4]It is recommended that contraction and release from the back lying position be learned first.

24

Contract as before. Remaining in the contraction, lower the body slowly backward toward the floor. The head is allowed to drop backward so that it moves toward the floor with the chin jutted forward. Arms continue to reach forward; knees remain slightly bent because of the tilt of the pelvis. Release the abdominal muscles, and the body becomes extended lying on the floor, arms at sides.

Split Sitting Position This position (also called stride, straddle, or second position) is accomplished by sitting on the floor with legs extended to the sides as far as possible (180° is the goal). The arms are extended to the sides parallel to the floor (also called second position), the back is straight, but the pelvis must not be tilted. Avoid locking the knees and do not allow the legs to rotate forward or backward.

I STRETCHES

FORWARD Lean gently forward from the hips. Alternate a given number of gentle stretches, keeping the back straight, with the same number of stretches with a

FIGURE 2-8
Split sitting position
E. Scott Lucia

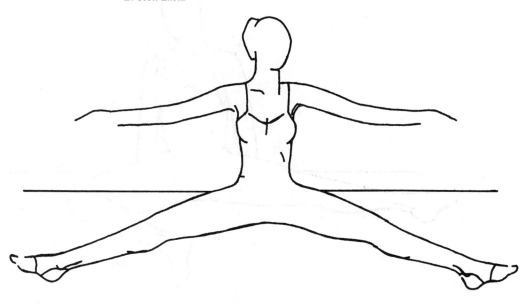

rounded back and head bent toward the floor. Do not return to upright sitting position until the desired sequence is finished.

SIDE Reach to one side and stretch the upright torso to that side. Repeat to the other side. Lifting the right arm over the head, bend the body to the left and slide the left hand along the left leg toward the ankle. Stretch gently several times. Alternate with several gentle stretches to the right. This can also be done with a twist of the torso by placing the left hand on the right knee while bending to the left with the right arm extended over the head. Stretch several times and then repeat to the other side. Or, twist the body to the left, reach toward the left ankle with both hands, and pull the head gently toward the knee. Stretch gently several pulses and repeat to the other side.

Forward and sideward stretches can also be done with one leg extended and the other knee bent with the leg folded close to the body either in front or in back. These positions are called half-split or jazz sit.

Stretches can be done in many different sequences; for example, stretch four to the left, four to the right, two

FIGURE 2-9
Half-split sitting position—front leg bent
E. Scott Lucia

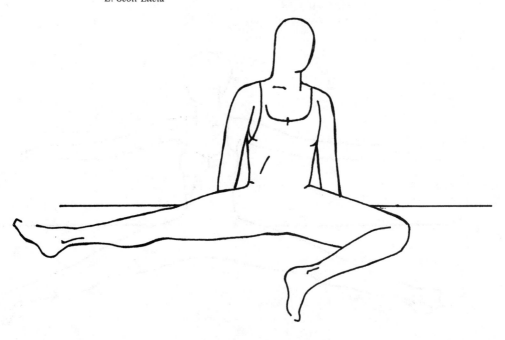

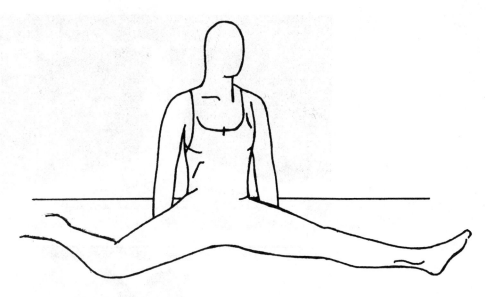

FIGURE 2-10
Half-split sitting position—leg extended in front
E. Scott Lucia

to the left, two to the right, one to the left, and one to the right. Or, stretch a given number of pulses to the left, to the center, to the right, to the center, to the left, and so on. Invent your own sequences. Find transitional movements of the arms to use when shifting from one stretch sequence to another.

2. ANKLE AND KNEE FLEXION AND EXTENSION

Sitting in split sitting position, alternately flex one ankle and extend the other. When the foot is flexed the heel is slightly off the floor. This can also be done by flexing both feet and then extending both feet. Now extend the right leg and foot. Flex the left ankle and bend the left knee. Alternate legs or do the exercise with both legs simultaneously.

3. CONTRACTION AND RELEASE

Sit with arms and legs in second position, back straight. Contract the abdominal muscles, rounding the back and dropping the head backward. The feet will flex and the arms will rotate so that the palms are supine and cupped. As the release of the abdominal muscles is accomplished,

FIGURE 2-11
Contraction in split
sitting position
Peter Krayer

FIGURE 2-12
Release in split sitting
position
Ken Roesser

bend forward from the hips so that as the back straightens it becomes parallel to the floor. The arms return to the original second position. Slowly return to upright sitting position. Other arm positions can also be experimented with during contraction and release.

4. CONTRACTION FROM TAILOR OR FROG SITTING POSITION TO RELEASE IN SPLIT SITTING POSITION

Begin in tailor or frog position. Contract as previously described and while in the contraction slowly slide the legs sideward and outward to split sitting position, keeping the feet flexed. As the release is accomplished, the body leans forward from the hips so that the back is flat and parallel to the floor, the arms rotate outward, and the feet are extended. Continue the movement of the trunk to split sitting position.

Long Sitting Position Sit on the floor with legs and feet extended, back straight, and arms at the sides.

FIGURE 2-13
Long sitting position
E. Scott Lucia

1 FORWARD STRETCHES

Stretch forward from the hips with back straight or from the waist with back rounded. Stretches can be done with extended or flexed feet. When the feet are flexed, the heels are off the floor. When stretching forward the arms reach toward or beyond the feet. Do not return to upright sitting position between stretches.

2. ANKLE FLEXION, EXTENSION, AND ROTATION

Remain in long sitting position. Extend the feet; flex the feet. Do this with both feet simultaneously or alternately. The knees can also flex as the feet flex. Rotate the foot from the ankle, inward, downward, outward, and upward. This can be done with both feet simultaneously, alternately, or in opposition. Remember to keep the back straight.

3. BACK FALL

It is advisable to learn falls from sitting or kneeling positions before attempting standing falls.

From long sitting position, raise the arms over the head, arch the back, extend the head backward. As the arms reach backward and outward toward the sides, the little fingers slide along the floor. The chest is held high as the top of the head first, and finally the back of the head, shoulders, and back, reach the floor. The recovery is accomplished by arching the back once again and lifting the body, chest first, to the sitting position. Continue the movement forward until the head drops over the knees, hands forward on the ankles. Complete the recovery by returning to the starting position.

Back Lying Position (supine)

Lie on the floor in a supine position with legs fully extended and arms at the sides or extended along the floor at shoulder height.

Any of the following exercises which involve the simultaneous lifting of both extended legs are not recommended for people with weak backs.

FIGURE 2-14
Back lying position
E. Scott Lucia

1 LEG LIFTING AND LOWERING

Begin with arms extended to the sides at shoulder height. Keeping both legs extended, lift the right leg until toes are pointing toward the ceiling. Lower slowly. Repeat with the left leg. The foot may be flexed or extended, depending on the desired muscle action.

2 HIP EXTENSIONS

From the back lying position with the arms extended to the sides at shoulder height, raise the extended right leg to the ceiling. Swing the leg outward toward the right side and attempt to touch the floor near the right hand. Slide the leg along the floor to starting position. Repeat with the left leg.

3. SPINE TWIST

Begin with arms extended to the sides at shoulder height. Keeping both legs extended, lift the right leg until toes are pointing toward the ceiling. Keeping both arms and shoulders on the floor, bring the right leg across the body, attempting to touch the left hand with the right toes. Lift the right leg toward the ceiling again and lower it to the floor. Repeat with the left leg.

4. LEG CIRCLES

In time, as more strength develops, the exercise may begin with extended legs. Lift both legs toward the ceiling. Keeping the legs extended, twist the body to the right and lower the legs toward the right side almost to the floor. Now swing the legs around in an arc to the left, still keeping the legs slightly off the floor. Then bring the legs back up toward the ceiling. Continue the circular motion of the legs.

5. CONTRACTION AND RELEASE[5]

The position of release is the back lying position with arms at sides. Contract the abdominal muscles. The contraction will cause other body movements to occur. The lower part of the pelvis will rotate upward. The back rounds slightly, the shoulders come forward, the arms reach forward with forearms and hands supine and palms cupped. The knees bend slightly, and the feet remain in contact with the floor. The neck is relaxed and the head drops backward. The lumbar region of the back is flat against the floor. Return to the release position with a strong motion. To determine whether you are contracting properly, place one hand on the floor under the lumbar region of the back while in the release position. Most of us will have a space between the floor and the back. As the contraction occurs, that space should fill in.

    The breathing for this and all other contractions is as follows: Inhale during the release. Exhale during the contraction.

---

[5]This contraction and release from the back lying position should be learned before contractions in other positions are attempted.

The contraction can also be done on the diagonal by bringing one shoulder forward diagonally toward the opposite leg and release to the original position.

The contraction from the back lying position can be terminated by a release in tailor, frog, or long sitting position. Then contract and return to back lying position. Release into original position.

6. INVERTED PLIÉ

Assume the back lying position with arms extended at shoulder height. Raise both extended legs to the ceiling. Rotate the legs outward. Flex the feet as if standing on the ceiling. Bend the knees. Extend the legs. Repeat. The feet can be extended and flexed between each plié.

7. BEATS

Assume the back lying position, arms extended at shoulder height. Raise both extended legs to the ceiling into third position with feet extended. The heel of one foot is against the instep of the other foot. Alternate the feet from right foot in front to left foot in front with quick little "beatlike" movements. Legs can remain extended toward the ceiling throughout or the legs can lower gradually to the floor and return to the ceiling as the "beats" continue.

8. ABDOMINAL STRENGTHENER

Lie on back with arms at sides. Keeping the back straight and flexing the body at the hips, reach with the arms toward the extended legs which are raised from the floor. The body is now in a V shape, balanced on the coccyx.

FIGURE 2-16
Abdominal strengthener
Marj Cox

Return to starting position. Repeat and hold the position for longer periods as the strength of the abdominal muscles increases.

9. LEG STRETCH

Lie on the back. Bend the right knee to the chest. Clasp both hands around the right leg just above the knee. Gently pull the bent knee toward the chest several times. Slowly extend the right leg until foot and leg are extended toward the ceiling. Now gently pull the extended leg toward the head with several gentle pulses. Also, flex and extend the foot while the leg is extended. Return the right leg to the floor and repeat with the left leg.

This can also be done with the foot flexed.

The above exercise can also be done without the use of the arms. Bend one leg, extend the leg toward the ceiling with extended or flexed foot, lower the leg.

FIGURE 2-17
Hook lying position
E. Scott Lucia

Both leg stretch exercises can be accomplished in hook lying position as well as supine position.

Prone Lying — Lie face down on the floor with arms at the sides. The head can rest on the forehead or the chin, or the face can be turned to one side resting on one cheek.

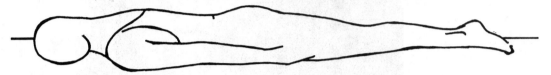

FIGURE 2-18
Prone lying position
E. Scott Lucia

1 LEG LIFTS

Bend the elbows and place the forearms on the floor so that the elbows are directly under the shoulders, palms facing one another. The back is arched and the chest is off the floor. Look straight ahead. The legs are extended and the tops of the feet rest on the floor. Lift the right leg straight up as high as possible without bending the knee or twisting the spine. Lower slowly with control. Repeat with the left leg.

2. LEG LIFT, BODY TWIST, AND EXTENSION

Lift the right leg as above. Continue the movement across the body to the left, bending the knee and finally placing the foot on the floor to the outside of the left leg. As the body twists, keep the arms on the floor until the foot is in place. Now the body follows the leg into a sitting position with the left leg extended and the left hand on the floor in back of the body. The right knee remains bent, the right elbow is bent and close to the medial side of the right knee, and the hand is pointing upward close to the head. Pushing on the left hand, extend the body upward and reach with the right arm toward the ceiling. The body now resembles an inclined plane.

Return to the seated position. Rotate the body to the left, place the arms on the floor as before, lift the right leg, and then slowly lower it to the starting position. The

FIGURE 2-19
Leg lift, body twist,
and extension
Marj Cox

technique should be done slowly with a sustained quality at first; later the tempo can increase and the quality can become percussive. Repeat on the other side.

3. LEG LIFT, BODY TWIST, AND STRETCH

Begin in the position as for the leg lift exercise. Lift the right leg. Keeping the arms on the floor, extend the leg across the body toward the left and bend the knee until the leg is on the floor. Follow with the body until reaching a half-split sitting position in which the right leg is folded back and the left leg is extended to the side. Stretch the arms toward the left foot, bringing the head toward the knee. Sit up, bringing the right arm forward, over the head, and backward. Follow with the body backward until the forearm rests on the floor. The body is now arched backward, and the legs remain as before. Sit up. Stretch again over the left leg. Sit up. Return the arms to the floor by twisting to the left. Lift the right leg. Lower slowly. Repeat the exercise with the left leg.

Side Lying

Side lying position is accomplished by lying on one side of the body, legs extended, one leg on top of the other. The bottom arm is extended over the head along the floor with the head resting on the arm; the top arm is extended downward along the top leg or the hand is placed on the floor in front of the chest.

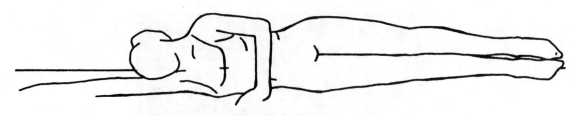

FIGURE 2-20 Side lying
E. Scott Lucia

1. LEG STRETCHES

PARALLEL Lying on the left side, bend the left elbow and prop the head on the palm. Place the right hand on the floor, palm down, in front of the chest. Keeping both legs extended and parallel, lift the right leg as high as possible with extended leg and foot. Slowly return the leg to starting position. Repeat as many times as desired. Roll over and repeat on the other side.

Repeat the exercise, lifting both legs from the floor while keeping the legs together and straight. Repeat on the other side.

TURNED OUT Repeat as above with the top leg turned out. As the top leg is extended toward the ceiling, the leg can be gently pulled toward the head with the free hand. Or, from the extended position toward the ceiling the foot can be flexed and extended.

2. LEG BEND AND STRETCH

Begin in side lying position on the left side with the left arm propping the head on bent elbow. Rotate the right leg to the turned-out position and touch the right toes to the left knee on count 1. On count 2 extend the right leg toward the ceiling. On count 3 return to the toes-to-knee position, and on count 4 return to starting position. Repeat on the other side.

Z Sitting Position Z sitting position (hurdle sit, side sit, fourth, or "on the walk") is accomplished by sitting in frog position, then bringing one leg around in back of the body with the knee bent. The back is straight; arms are at the sides. The front foot is "on the walk," which means that if one were to turn it over it would be ready to walk. The heel is downward but not touching the floor. The two "sitting bones" (tuberosities of the ischia) are in contact with the floor. Many students find it difficult to contact the floor with both tuberosities.

1 TWIST

Sitting in Z position with the left leg in front, raise the arms to shoulder height and round them slightly forward. Twist to the left, extending the left foot and raising the body so that the right hip is off the floor while maintaining an upright torso. The twist originates in the hips, followed by the waist and then the shoulders. The head follows the upper body. Return to starting position.

The exercise can be varied by opening the arms as follows. As the body twists to the left, the left arm is brought forward in front of the face and raised over the head and extended to the left. As the body returns to center, the left arm slashes back across the front of the body with the palm upturned and the arm at chest height. Meanwhile, the right arm during the twist is slashed across in front of the body and during the return opens over the head and to the side.

FIGURE 2-21
Z sitting twist
with open arms
Marj Cox

To change sides when sitting in Z position with the left leg in front, extend both legs to the right and support the body on the left hand. Swing the legs around to the front and to the left, now supporting the body on the right hand. Then fold the legs into the Z on the opposite side. This change is accomplished to the count of 3.

2. TWIST AND BACKWARD STRETCH

Begin in Z position with left leg in front. Twist to the left. As you return to center, extend the right arm over the head. Keeping the arm semiflexed, continue the arm movement toward the floor on the right as the body follows until the forearm is resting on the floor. The back arches as it follows the arm. The left arm follows and is raised in front of the face in an arc. Recover by swinging the arms and body forward in a circle close to the floor, over the legs, and toward the left and upward. Change legs to alternate Z sitting position and repeat.

Kneeling Position The kneeling position is accomplished simply by kneeling on both knees, keeping the body straight and the arms at the sides. Some students find it painful to remain on the knees for more than a few minutes, so kneeling exercises, especially at first, should be limited in number or performed with knee pads.

FIGURE 2-22
Kneeling position
E. Scott Lucia

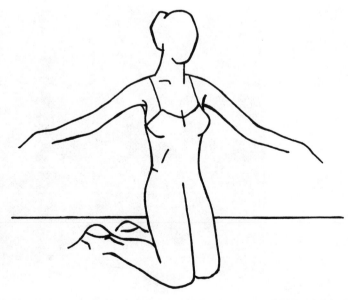

1 LEAN

Keeping the torso absolutely straight, lean backward from the knees and return to starting position. The arms can remain at the sides or can reach forward with straight arms and upturned palms. The head remains in a straight line with the torso throughout.

2. SIDE SIT

From the kneeling position, bring both arms over the head, slightly rounded. Keeping the upper body erect, sit on the floor to the left of the legs. Return to kneeling. Sit to the right of the legs and return.

3. SIDE EXTENSIONS

From the kneeling position, crouch over the knees and place the hands on the floor in front of the knees. Now place the left hand on the floor about two feet to the left of the legs. When doing this, lean the body to the left and bring the right arm across in front of the face until it is extended over the head and at the same time extend the right leg to the right side. The body is now supported by the left hand and the left knee. The toes of the right foot are on the floor. To recover, bring the right leg back to kneeling position as the right arm returns in front of the body and the upper body returns to crouched position over the knees. Pressure on the left hand gives the force to accomplish this movement. Repeat to the right side.

When you have mastered the above, repeat with the following variation. As the leg is extended, lift it as high off the floor as possible.

4. FALLS

FRONT From the kneeling position, keeping the body rigid, lean forward and as the body falls toward the floor check the movement by placing the left hand on the floor near the chest and sliding the right hand, weight on the little finger, forward until the arm is fully extended. As the body falls to the floor the legs are extended in back of the body. The recovery is done by bending at the hips and bringing the body back to the kneeling position.

BACK From the kneeling position, with arms at the sides, lean backward and as the body falls extend the arms to the sides and slide the little fingers outward and backward along the floor. As the body falls to the floor, the weight is caught first on one hip and then the legs are extended. The recovery occurs by lifting the chest, raising the upper body, folding the legs at the knees, and returning to the kneeling position.

SIDE From the kneeling position, the body leans toward the right side. Place the left hand on the floor in front of the chest and slide the right arm to the right to full extension and straighten the legs. Use the little finger as the contact with the floor. To recover, press on the left hand, lift the body, and return to the kneeling position. Repeat to the left side.

These front, back, and side falls can be done in succession using a specific number of counts for each fall and each recovery.

5. CONTRACTION AND RELEASE ON ALL FOURS

From the position commonly described as on all fours, contract the abdominal muscles, allowing the back to round and the head to drop, chin to chest. Release by releasing the abdominals, straightening the back, and returning to the original position. The hands and knees remain in the starting position throughout.

FIGURE 2-23
On all fours
E. Scott Lucia

40

FIGURE 2-24
Contraction and release
with arched back
Marj Cox

6. CONTRACTION AND RELEASE WITH ARCHED BACK

From the kneeling position, lean forward until the back is as flat as a table and reach back and grasp the achilles tendons with the index and middle fingers. The head should be in line with the back, and the eyes look down at the floor. If you do not have a mirror, have someone check this starting position because it is difficult to feel kinesthetically. The starting position is the position of release. Contract the abdominal muscles. The back rounds, the shoulders come forward slightly, and the head drops forward. The hips move backward slightly as if to sit on the heels, but not quite. The fingers remain on the achilles tendons. Release by releasing the abdominals, pushing the hips forward, arching the back, and dropping the head backward. The fingers remain as before, and the arms are fully extended. Contract as before. Release to the starting position.

7. CONTRACTION AND RELEASE WITH ROLLS

Following the contraction and release with arched back, contract again as before. Remaining in the contraction and keeping the elbows tucked in close to the body and the fingers on the achilles tendons, roll to the right. Release while returning to an upright position. Now repeat the contraction, roll to the left, and release.

From the kneeling position, sit to the left of the legs. Raise the arms to the sides at chest height. Even though the body is somewhat "scoliotic" because of sitting on only one hip, compensate and make the upper body straight, with shoulders parallel to the floor. This starting position is the position of release. Contract the abdominal muscles, allow the head to drop back, and, turning the arms upward, bring them forward slightly. Release strongly to the starting position. Contract a second time; reach back and to the sides with the arms and, keeping the little fingers in contact with the floor, do a back fall while maintaining the abdominal contraction. The release is now accomplished by releasing the abdominals, hyperextending the back, and supporting the body on the left arm which has been brought in along the left side of the body. The body rests on the left shoulder, along the arm, and on the bent left leg. The rest of the body is arched and held off the floor. The right arm has been flung forward across the body in front of the face and is now reaching backward over the head. Contract the abdominals and double the body forward over the knees, which have been brought together and are now on the floor. This position causes the body to rotate one-eighth turn to the left. Release by straightening the torso over the legs and slowly raising the torso to the starting position.

Standing   You have learned how to stand correctly in a natural position with feet parallel. It is important to understand and experience the turned-out leg positions of classical ballet as well. The five positions of the arms and legs were named by Pierre Beauchamp around 1700. With some modifications they have remained in use to this day. Early modern dancers who rebelled against the rigidity of ballet shunned the turned-out leg and the pointed foot. Instead they stood with parallel feet and often extended a leg with a flexed foot. Some innovative ballet choreographers such as Nijinsky and Fokine also experimented with these

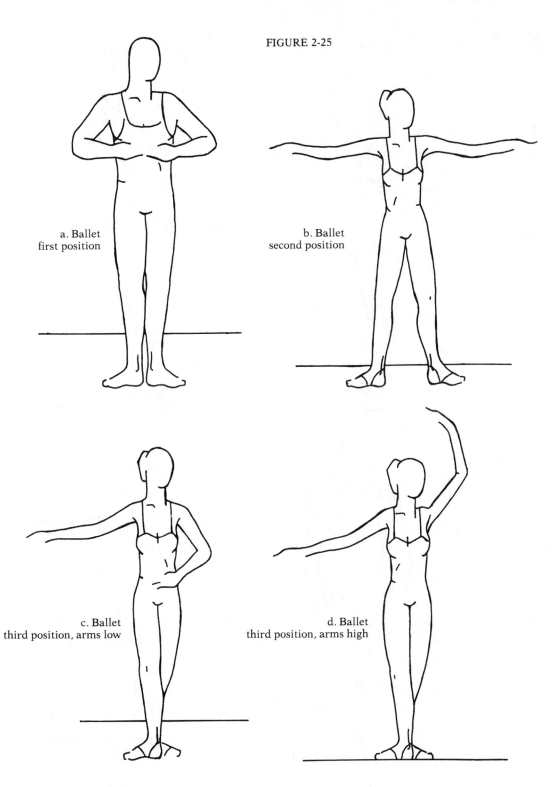

FIGURE 2-25

a. Ballet
first position

b. Ballet
second position

c. Ballet
third position, arms low

d. Ballet
third position, arms high

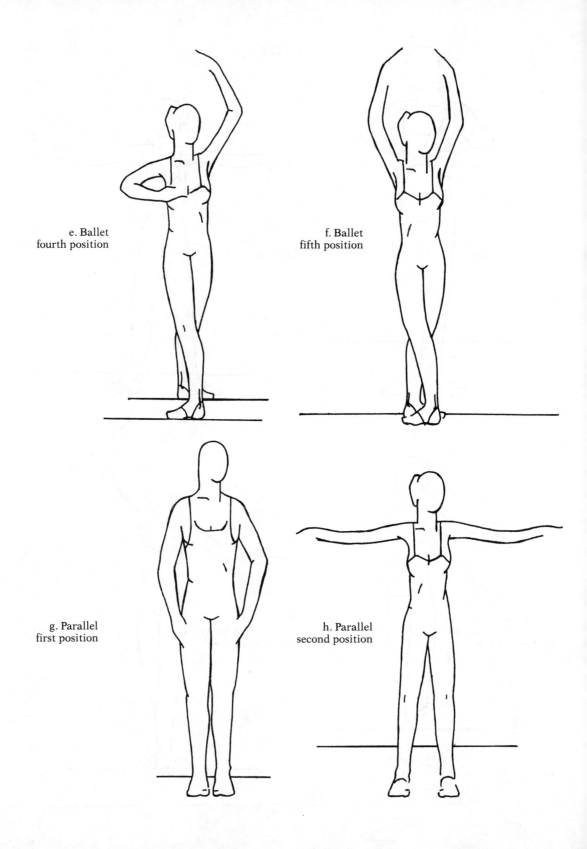

e. Ballet
fourth position

f. Ballet
fifth position

g. Parallel
first position

h. Parallel
second position

"natural" movements. Now the lines are not so rigid between the styles of dance, and we find that ballet positions and techniques have been accepted in the vocabulary of movement of modern dance, jazz dance, and even some ethnic styles, so great has been the influence of Mr. Beauchamp's rules.

Some of the following exercises begin in parallel standing positions and others in "ballet" positions.

1 STANDING RELAXATION

From a stride standing position,[6] slowly drop the head, arms, and upper body toward the floor, bending at the waist and keeping the knees straight. Relax in this position.

Slowly return by starting from the lower spine, "one vertebra after another." The head is the last to return to the upright standing position. In yoga practice this is called the refresher, and it is indeed just that. It can be done before the stretches which follow to gently warm up the spine. It is also useful at the end of a strenuous class.

2. STRETCHES

DOWN AND UP   Standing in a comfortable stride position, feet slightly turned out, lean forward from the waist and hips until the head and arms are hanging downward toward the floor. Relax gently toward the floor a designated number of times. Return to upright standing and stretch the extended right arm to the ceiling, now the left, and again the right and the left. The feet remain flat on the floor, and the knees remain straight throughout. Alternatively try bending the left knee as the right arm stretches and vice versa.

SIDE   From an erect stride standing position, extend the right arm over the head and bend the body to the left, letting the left arm slide down the left side of the body. Do not allow the body to bend forward or backward. Stretch gently to the left a given number of times. Repeat to the

---

[6]Stride standing usually implies slightly abducted legs.

right an equal number of times. For variety, extend both arms over the head during the stretch.

FORWARD AND BACKWARD From the stride standing position, extend the arms outward to the sides at shoulder height. Keeping the back straight and the head in line with the back, lean forward from the hips, and stretch gently the desired number of times. The legs remain straight. Return to upright standing, lean backward, and, placing the hands on the hips, stretch gently backward an equal number of times. It may be necessary to bend the knees slightly as the body bends backward.

SIDE TWIST From the upright stride standing position with arms extended at shoulder height, twist from the hips and waist to the left a given number of times. Repeat to the right.

SIDE LUNGE From the upright stride standing position with arms extended at shoulder height, plié the left knee, keeping the body facing front and the right leg straight. Alternate several pliés with the left leg with several pliés with the right leg.

SIDE LUNGE WITH TWIST   The previously described exercise can be done with a twist of the body to the left as the left plié is accomplished. Bring the right arm across in front of the body and push to the left with each plié. Repeat to the right.

These stretches can be accomplished in many different sequences. Choose music or percussive accompaniment to fit the desired rhythm. Invent transitional movements to flow smoothly from one sequence to the next.

3. RIB CAGE MOBILITY

Standing with arms extended to the sides at shoulder height, move the rib cage to one side without moving the hips, shoulders or arms. Return the rib cage to center. If this is difficult to do, place the left hand on the left side of the ribs and the right hand on the right side of the hips. Push the ribs to the right. Now reverse hand positions for the push back to center and to the left. At first it may be helpful to watch the rib cage movement in a mirror.

4. CONTRACTION AND RELEASE

Stand with feet parallel and comfortably apart. The arms are held in second position. Contract the abdominals, rounding the back slightly so that the pelvis tips forward and upward and the shoulders come forward. The neck is relaxed, and the head may drop either forward or backward. Release strongly and return to starting position.

5. BRUSHES

Brushes are similar to the *battement tendu* in ballet. Brushes are accomplished from an erect standing position, usually with arms extended at shoulder height, held at the sides, or, if being done with one leg only, in third position with the arm opposite to the working leg held in front of the body. Exercises requiring that the weight be supported on one leg while the other leg is in motion frequently cause a balance problem. You may rest one hand gently on a ballet barre, the wall, the edge of a stage, a chair, or a partner until sufficient balance is developed to practice these exercises without support.

PARALLEL Standing as above with feet parallel, keeping both knees straight, slide the right foot forward, extending the foot and keeping the toes in contact with the floor. The foot is now strongly arched. Slide the foot back to standing position and return the weight to the foot. Brushes should be done smoothly but precisely. They can be done successively a given number of times with each foot, or they can be done with alternate feet.

The brush motion can be carried forward beyond the reach of the toes until the fully extended leg is lifted off the floor. At first the lift should be only a few inches off the floor; later the elevation can be increased. Be sure that the knee remains straight throughout and that the only flexion of the body is in the hip joint. As the leg is lifted, do not allow the waist to bend forward as in a football kick. As the leg returns to the floor, the toes touch first and the foot brushes back to standing position. Brushes properly done produce a "swishing" sound on the floor.

FIRST POSITION   Brushes are done as described above, but with legs turned out and the knee in line with the toes. The turnout will generally be approximately forty-five degrees. The brush is to the side. Be sure that the brush is done in the line of the foot. Brushes can also be done from first position to front and to back and from third position in any of the above mentioned directions.

6. FOOT EXTENSION

Stand with feet parallel and arms raised to the side at shoulder height. Lift the right heel off the floor so that the ball of the foot remains on the floor (count 1). This is called half toe. Continue the extension of the foot so that the top of the big toe is in contact with the floor (count 2, full toe). Return to half toe on count 3 and to starting position on count 4. Repeat with the other foot.

7. HEEL RAISING (RELEVÉ)

The relevé is a rising up on the toes. From parallel standing position, feet nearly together, lift the heels so that the body weight is on the balls of the feet and the toes. This is a sustained movement. If you have trouble with balance, focus your eyes on a stationary spot. You may use a barre for support at first. Return to standing position, again using a sustained movement.

The relevé can also be practiced in second position parallel or in the ballet positions. The relevé often follows the plié.

8. PEDALING (TREADING)

Standing with feet together and parallel and arms raised to the sides at shoulder height, bend the right knee, and lift the right heel off the floor; extend the foot so that only the tip of the big toe remains in contact with the floor. The supporting leg is kept straight. As the right foot and leg return to starting position, the left foot is extended, and the knee bends in order to alternate "pedaling" with the left and the right. At first the rhythm of the pedaling is slow and steady, but after the movement is mastered the rhythm can increase in tempo or can alternate between

FIGURE 2-26
Pedaling (left) and
prancing (right)
Marj Cox

fast and slow. Pedaling can also be done as a locomotor movement. As the foot is extended, push the leg forward slightly, keeping the tip of the big toe in contact with the floor. Repeat. Each "pedal" will move the body slightly forward.

9. PRANCING

Prancing involves the same motion as pedaling except that the bent knee is now lifted to a ninety-degree angle with the body; the foot is lifted well off the floor. As the foot is brought back to the floor, contact is made first by the top of the big toe, then the ball of the foot, and lastly the heel. As in pedaling, the left leg lifts as the right leg returns to the floor. Prancing should be done slowly at first, and then the tempo can be increased until prancing actually becomes leaplike, with moments when both feet are off the floor. Prancing can be done in place or can become a locomotor movement with movement forward. Prancing can be varied by lifting the bent knee to the sides or by lifting the leg behind the body with a slightly bent knee. When prancing is done vigorously, there must be a slight plié when landing.

The plié (from the French *plier*, "to bend") was originally associated with ballet, but because it is an excellent exercise for preparing the legs for jumping and strenuous activities, it has become a part of the preparation for modern dance and other dance forms. The plié can be accomplished from any of the five ballet positions and also from parallel positions. Modern dance classes most commonly utilize first and second in both parallel and turned-out positions. The technique is the same, regardless of the starting position. The knees and ankles bend slowly; the quality of the movement is sustained. As the knees bend and the body lowers, remember to lift the chest and feel a sense of reaching upward with the head as if suspended from the ceiling like a marionette. In ballet class, pliés are done with one hand on the barre for support. If you wish to use the barre, be sure that your hand rests lightly and that you do not distort your erect body position by leaning toward the barre. The body returns to starting position as the ankles and the knees are extended. There must be no forward, backward, or sideward movement of the torso or

FIGURE 2-27
Demi-plié
Ken Roesser

the head. It is important to think of oneself in a tight-fitting box or a narrow elevator shaft: as the body lowers and rises, there is no room to stick out in the seat or bend forward from the waist. One must be especially cautious when working in the turned-out positions. In an effort to go lower, there is danger of compromising the body position. The turnout comes from the hips, not the knees or ankles. The feet must be directly under and in line with the knees. The feet must not pronate.

In mid-eighteenth-century France a machine called the *tourne-hanche*, or hip turner, was used by ballet students. The device mechanically forced the feet into a turned-out position without regard for anatomical readiness. We know better now. Beginners usually find that their feet and legs are turned out at only about forty-five degrees, and they should not attempt more at first. Pliés must be done in a slow, controlled manner. If they are done to a four-count beat, be sure to distribute the entire four counts evenly during the execution of the plié, rather than reaching your destination on counts 1 or 2.

DEMI-PLIÉ In a demi-plié, the bend of the ankles and knees occurs while the heels remain on the floor.

GRAND-PLIÉ The grand plié is accomplished by executing the demi-plié and then, when the legs can bend no farther, the heels are lifted and the legs continue to bend. It is important not to lose the feeling of lift as the body is lowered. The tendency to "sit" must be avoided. As the extension of the legs occurs, the heels are replaced on the floor when appropriate, and the extension continues as in a demi-plié. In ballet second position the heels do not rise during the grand-plié.

During the plié, the arms can be held in one position or moved from low to center or high or to the sides. It is important that the carriage of the arms be planned to enhance the balance of the body as well as the appearance.

Combinations of pliés from different starting positions and also combinations of the plié and relevé are useful to add variety to the daily practice. Here is one example; you can invent others. Begin in second position (turned out). Plié (count 1). From the bent position of the legs, switch the weight to the left leg and straighten the right leg (count 2). Return to second position plié with weight centered (count 3). Switch to the right-leg plié with the left leg straight (count 4). Return again to second position plié (count 5). Return to starting position (count 6).

Invent transitional movement when changing from plié in one position to plié in another.

II. EXTENSIONS

There are several ways to prepare the leg muscles for extensions. From a standing position with feet parallel or in ballet first position and arms raised to the sides at shoulder height, slowly bend the right knee and lift the leg to a ninety-degree angle. Keep the foot extended. Slowly extend the knee until the leg is straight and parallel to the floor. Bend the knee and return the foot to the floor. Repeat with the left leg. This can also be done by holding the leg just above the knee with both hands; or the leg can be lifted while fully extended until it is perpendicular to the

FIGURE 2-28
Leg extension (forward)
Ken Roesser

FIGURE 2-29
Leg extension (sideward)
Marj Cox

body. This is similar to a brush with high elevation or to a *grand battement* in ballet. Extensions are possible to the front or to the back from a parallel stance. When extending to the back, however, the knee must be bent slightly if the leg is to be lifted very high. Extensions can be done to the sides from a turned-out position or diagonally forward from a semi–turned-out stance. When starting with the legs turned out, the leg is extended to the side and the knee is facing the ceiling.

12. LEG EXTENSION WITH LIFT

Extend the right leg forward and upward until it is perpendicular to the body (count 1). Hold on count 2. Lift the leg slightly higher on counts 3, 4, and 5. Return the leg to the floor on count 6. Repeat with the left leg.

This can also be accomplished from a turned-out leg position.

13. JUMPS IN PLACE

"Little jumps in place," as they are often called, can be accomplished from any upright standing position: parallel or turned-out. The jumps start with a slight plié, and as

FIGURE 2-30
Frog jump
Marj Cox

the body lifts into the air the legs and feet are fully extended. The landing takes place first on the toes, then the whole foot, and then into a plié. Jumps can take off from one position and land in another. For example, start in first position, land in second. Take off from second, land in first. Or, jump three times facing front, turn one quarter turn to the right on count 4. Repeat until you return to front. Try other kinds of jumps also—split jump (as in Russian folk dances), stag jump, frog jump, cheerleader jump, etc. When many jumps are repeated in succession, it is sometimes helpful to chant, count, or recite nonsensical rhymes while jumping to avoid shortness of breath. At first, jumps can be practiced facing and holding the barre with both hands. Avoid leaning into the barre.

14. ACHILLES OR HAMSTRING STRETCH

Stand facing a barre or wall with hands on the support. Extend the right leg backward and place the foot on the floor on half toe. Bend the supporting leg. Stretch the right leg and dorsiflex the ankle gently until the heel is flat on the floor. Repeat several times. Alternate legs.

Achilles tendon stretches can also be done without a wall or barre by bending forward from the waist, bending the knees, and placing both palms on the floor. Now slowly extend the knees and hold. Bend the knees. Extend again. Hands remain on the floor throughout.

15. ARM SWINGS (PENDULAR SWINGS)

SIDE TO SIDE Stand in a comfortable stride with the feet partially turned out and the arms hanging loosely at the sides. Swing both arms to the left. The body weight shifts to the left leg, and only the toes of the right foot are now in contact with the floor. Now swing the arms to the right in a downward arc; as the body follows to be centered over the right foot, there is a slight plié of the legs. Repeat this down-up side-to-side motion several times. You will find a three-beat rhythm most appropriate for each swing. There should be an easy "hang loose" feeling of the body during the movement, although the body reaches a full extension at the height of each swing.

SIDE AND CIRCLE   Start with the arms reaching to the left, swing them down and to the right (count 1), swing to the left (count 2), swing to the right, and continue the arms upward and around over the head and back to the right side (counts 3 and 4). Now repeat the sequence from the new starting position (arms at the right).

SIDE AND CIRCLE WITH SIDE STEP   Repeat the sequence above. As the arms circle (on counts 3 and 4), step sideward to the right on the right foot (count 3), close the left foot to the right foot (count "and"). Step again to the right with the right foot and remain with the weight of the body centered over the right foot (count 4). Repeat to the left.

SIDE AND CIRCLE WITH TURN   Repeat as above except, as the right foot steps to the right, rotate clockwise on the foot to face the rear; as the body continues the rotation towards the front, hop from the right foot to the left foot and then step on the right foot again as in the original version of the exercise. The arms circle as before during the body rotation. You are now facing in the same direction as in the beginning.

DOWN AND UP   Stand with feet parallel and about twelve inches apart. Extend the arms forward to shoulder height. Plié, dropping the head, arms, and body downward. The arms continue to move backward as the legs straighten. The back is slightly rounded, and the eyes look downward toward the floor. Plié again and return the arms forward and upward as the legs and the body straighten. There is a "down-up, down-up" feeling to this movement, and it can be counted "1 and 2" or "1, 2, 3; 1, 2, 3."

16. ARM-AND-LEG SWINGS

FORWARD AND BACKWARD   Start with the weight on the right foot and the left toes on the floor slightly to the rear. Both arms are raised to shoulder height; the left arm is extended forward and the right to the side. As the left swings forward, the arms swing in opposition so that now the right arm is forward and the left is to the side (count 1). Continue the leg swing to the rear with arm swing to the opposite position (count 2). On count 3 the left leg swings forward and the arms change position. On count 4 both feet touch the floor and the weight is on both feet in preparation for the swing of the right leg. The arms remain still on count 4.

In each instance the leg swings freely from the hip, the foot brushes the floor as it swings forward and backward, and the knee is free to bend slightly. The arms touch the sides of the body during the transition from one position to another.

SIDEWARD Stand with arms raised to shoulder height, swing the right leg with bent knee upward and inward across the body, then swing downward brushing the floor, and finally extend the leg outward to the right side. Repeat, brushing the floor with the foot on each transition from center to side. Arms remain in place.

Falls When discussing differences between modern dance and classical ballet, people often comment on the fact that ballet is an aerial form of dance which emphasizes elevation of the dancers *en pointe* and in jumps and leaps, whereas modern dance is more concerned with "earthiness" as evidenced by falling to the floor. Whether or not this comparison is valid, it is certainly true that modern dancers have utilized all levels of space: high, low, and in between. Much of Doris Humphrey's technique is based on the fall and recovery. In any school of modern dance one is soon introduced to the technique of falling and recovering in several different ways. Whether in learned falls or one's own improvised falls, one must always remember that even when appearing to relax and fall limply to the floor there must be muscular control to prevent injury. One must avoid landing on the knees, elbows, coccyx, and, of course, head. Other parts of the body are more "padded" and therefore able to absorb the landing. One is advised to learn falls from a sitting or kneeling position before attempting standing falls.

1 SWINGING SIDE FALL
(To the Right)

Begin in stride standing position with both arms reaching to the left. Swing the arms and body to the right (count 1). Swing the arms and body to the left, and pick up the right leg and bend it backward and laterally (count 2). Swing the body and arms to the right, lowering the body by bending the (left) supporting leg. As the body is lowered and falls toward the floor, catch it with the left palm on the floor in front of the chest and slide the right arm (little finger on the floor) to the right until it is fully extended. The top of the right foot is on the floor behind the left foot, and the right leg extends as the body lands on the right hip. (*Caution:* The right knee does not come in contact with the floor.) The body is gradually lowered to an extended position on the right side, both legs extended. After the fall, the left leg may be elevated to a diagonal position. The right arm is extended along the floor, and the left hand remains on the floor in front of the chest (counts 3 and 4).

To recover, on count 1, push on the left hand, swing the body to the left, and step on the left foot as the body is raised slightly off the floor. On count 2, step on the right foot as the body and arms swing to the right. By now you are nearly at standing level. Count 3 completes the upward motion as arms and body swing again to the left. On count

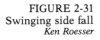

FIGURE 2-31
Swinging side fall
Ken Roesser

4, swing to the right. You are now in position to repeat the fall to the left.

2. SWINGING BACK FALL

Stand in second position parallel, arms extended to the front at shoulder height. Swing the body and arms downward with a small plié, then upward with torso parallel to the floor and arms reaching to back (counts "and 1"). Plié and swing down and then up to full standing position *en relevé* with arms extended over the head ("and 2"). Repeat the above ("and 3, and 4"). This time, as the body reaches full extension on count 4, raise the right leg and bend the knee laterally. Plié and swing downward, lowering the body. Reach backward toward the floor with both arms and land on the seat and the hands, which slide out along the floor over the head. The right leg remains folded behind the extended left leg (counts "and 5, and 6"). Avoid landing on the knee. To recover, lift the body, chest leading and hands sliding forward along the floor. Bend forward until the weight is on both feet (knees are bent) ("and 7"). Swing upward to full extension ("and 8"). The fall may now be repeated with the left leg bent in back.

3. PERCUSSIVE BACK FALL

Stand in a wide solid stride. Count 1: Reach back with the extended left arm and reach toward the ceiling with the extended right arm. Count 2: With the weight centered in the thighs, bend backward and place the palm of the left hand on the floor. You are now supported on two feet and one hand. Count 3: Rotate the body toward the left until the right hand is on the floor, and kick both legs straight up into the air. For a moment you are in a handstand. Counts "and 4": As the legs come down, land on the toes of one foot first and then the other, and as the feet contact the floor allow the legs to slide backward. (The weight is mostly on the hands during this time.)

You are now lying in an extended prone position. To recover, on count 1, rotate to the right as you assume a sitting position with the right leg bent at the knee, the right foot flat on the floor, and the left leg extended. The right elbow is bent and held next to the inside of the right

FIGURE 2-32
Percussive back fall
Marj Cox

knee; the left arm is extended diagonally to the rear with the palm on the floor. On count 2, push the body into a full extension, raising the body from the floor; balance on the extended left arm, the bent right leg, and the extended left leg. Reach toward the ceiling with the right arm. On count 3, place both feet on the floor and bring the body to an upright but crouched position. On counts "and 4," spring upward into the air and land on both feet in the original standing position.

4. ARM AND SHOULDER BACK FALL

Stand in a solid parallel stride position with arms at the sides. Raise the right arm forward, upward, and backward as the body leans backward and the weight is lowered "into" the thighs. As the knees continue to bend, the weight is supported by the thigh muscles. As the right arm reaches back toward the floor, first touch the little finger to the floor and slide the hand, arm, and shoulder backward as the feet slide forward. The contact with the floor should be smooth and gradual. You are now in a back lying

FIGURE 2-33
Arm and shoulder back fall
Marj Cox

position with the right arm extended over the head along the floor. To recover, bend the left knee, keep the right leg extended, and roll backward to the shoulders. Then roll forward onto both feet and stand. This fall can also be done without the extended arm. The shoulder contacts the floor first instead of the hand and arm.

5. CIRCULAR FALL

Stand in a wide stride, arms rounded toward the front and at chest level. Twist from the waist to the right (this is the windup). Now twist to the left, lowering the body by bending the knees. As the body lowers, catch the weight on the hand of the extended left arm then on the left hip. Meanwhile, bring the right arm across the face in a semicircle over the head and slide it along the floor until it is reaching backward. The left arm also slides along the floor until it is reaching backward over the head. The body now rests on the left shoulder, the left side, and the outside of the left leg. Both legs are now bent backward and separated at the knees. The body is inverted backward in a "shrimplike" position.

To recover, the right arm retraces its path along the floor over the head and to the front. The body weight is lifted by the left hand and is gradually brought forward onto both feet. As the body rises, the circular motion is continued to the right. Continue turning several times as you return to standing position. Then continue the rota-

FIGURE 2-34
Circular fall
Ken Roesser

FIGURE 2-35
Half-split fall
Marj Cox

tional motion of both arms as they are extended over the head. Let the motion gradually diminish.

6. HALF-SPLIT FALL

From a stride standing position, extend the right arm and right leg to the side. Simultaneously pivot to the left on the left foot. Bend the left knee, place the extended right foot on the floor, and slide downward into a half split. Reach backward with the right hand to catch the body weight. The left arm is extended over the head.

There are several ways to recover. One way is to place the left hand on the floor to the right of the body while rolling into a prone position. Lift the body with both arms, step forward on the left foot, and stand. The fall can be done to the other side by reversing these instructions.

7. FORWARD FALL

This fall is not recommended unless the arms and shoulders are fairly strong. Those who have done push-ups will have no trouble with it. Stand with legs partially turned out. Let the feet slide sideward into or toward a split

FIGURE 2-36
Forward fall
Marj Cox

position as the body leans forward. Catch the weight on the hands in front of the chest.

There are several possible recoveries from this fall. One way is to roll over toward the left until in a half-split sitting position with the right leg bent and the left leg straight and extended to the side. Stand by stepping on the left foot to the right of the right bent leg and then step on the right foot.

The falls presented here originate from a relatively stable base. Locomotor falls, while fascinating to watch and interesting to learn, are for more advanced students because of a higher chance of injury. When falling to the floor from a moving base, there is the possibility of slipping, tripping, or losing control and landing on an unplanned body part. Until body control is quite well developed, stationary falls are recommended.

Chapter 3 introduces the components of movement and offers suggestions for problem solving through movement exploration. These and other improvisational opportunities will enable you to develop the freedom to use your prepared instrument in new ways.

3

THE ELEMENTS OF
MOVEMENT
SPACE, TIME, AND FORCE

Movement is the medium of dance. The elements of movement are space, time, and force. A dancer must become familiar with the interaction of the various components of each of these elements of movement. This is accomplished by exploring how the body moves in and through space, learning how time factors affect motion or stillness, and by experiencing the influence of the effects of energy on muscular exertion. The three elements are separated only for purposes of analysis, for they are in reality inseparable; each influences and is influenced by the others.

SPACE Space is the area which surrounds us. It is the environment in which we live and breathe, and in dance it is the area in which we move in order to produce patterns and designs. In dance class, space is defined by and limited by the walls, floor, and ceiling of the studio or gymnasium.

We can simplify our understanding of movement in space by defining the part of the body that supports us at any one time as the base. Movement of the body in relation to the base is described as locomotor or axial.

Base LOCOMOTOR MOVEMENT

Locomotor movement is movement in which the body travels *through* space by constantly changing the base of support. Usually the base consists of the feet, but this is not always the case; one can "locomote" through space in other ways. For example, locomotion may occur on one's knees, on one hand and one foot, or on both hands.

Let us first examine the eight movements generally considered to be the basic locomotor movements which

FIGURE 3-1
Locomotor movement (leap)
Peter Krayer

utilize the feet as the base and which form the foundation for most dance movements. Later you will see how they can be varied and how new means of locomotion can be devised. These movements are all natural ways of locomoting from one place to another which we learned as children, and most of us never consider the technical analysis of how they are accomplished. Although the major thrust of this analysis is the feet and legs, the rest of the body is also important. The torso must be controlled. The arms must either swing in opposition to the legs or be held in a specific position. Avoid allowing the arms to just dangle in monkey fashion. And, most important of all, do not forget focus! Look where you are going, not at the floor!

I WALK

The walk is accomplished by transferring the weight from one foot to another in an even rhythm. There are endless variations on the way one can walk; the simplest is as if going from one place to another without thought of the mechanics of walking. One can also walk in a stylized dance walk, starting in demi-plié and contacting the floor toes first and legs turned out. Straight-legged, duck-footed, inverted, everted, or tiptoed are other possibilities for varying the techniques of walking. One can walk forward, backward, sideward, or in any direction. The tempo of the walk can be moderate, fast, or slow; the rhythm, though usually even, is sometimes made uneven as in a limp. Walks are generally done to $\frac{2}{4}$ or $\frac{4}{4}$ time.

The arms swing in opposition to the legs in a normal walk. To stylize the walk, try swinging the arms in synchrony with the leg on the same side or eliminate the arm swing by holding the arms in a fixed position.

Other walk variations:

Walk forward four steps, backward two steps, and continue this pattern across the floor.

Starting on the right foot, walk forward eight steps, backward four steps, turn sharply to the right, and walk forward two steps, backward two steps, turn to face in the original line of direction, and repeat.

Starting with the left foot, walk forward eight steps with arms swinging in opposition. Turn to the open side (left) and continue to walk four steps, again turn to the open side (left) and walk two steps, turn (left) and walk two steps again, turn (left) and step once, and bring the other foot to place.

Invent your own combination of walk variations as you move across the floor.

2. RUN

When running, the transfer of weight is from one foot to the other, with a slight suspension in the air between steps. The toes and the ball of the foot generally contact the floor first, the knees are slightly bent throughout, and the knees and ankles are flexible. The body leans forward slightly, and the arms are often held at waist height with elbows flexed rather than swinging freely in opposition. The rhythmic pattern of a run is even. The energy release varies according to the purpose of the run. Metrically, a run can be represented as follows, as well as in other ways.

$\frac{2}{4}$ run run run run | or $\frac{6}{8}$ run run run run run run

Running is done for speed, for distance, or in combination with other locomotor activities as in "run, run, leap."

Suggestions:

Try running for speed, to cover space and low to the ground, or picking up the feet as in a prance.

Practice running and stopping suddenly, starting suddenly, and changing directions abruptly.

Run halfway across the floor in a forward direction and, without losing speed and momentum, turn suddenly and continue to run in the same direction backwards.

3. LEAP

A leap is an extended run. The takeoff is from one foot and the landing is on the other. The energy can be expended so that the leap is for height or for distance, but either way the body is suspended in the air longer than in the run. The legs can be partially bent or fully extended as in the grand jeté. A leap requires a great deal of energy and is physically demanding. Try continuous leaps across the floor and you will understand why leaps are generally performed in combination with other activities. Run-leap is an effective way to practice leaping with one leg only. Run-run-leap provides an opportunity to leap on alternate legs. This is sometimes a difficult coordination for beginners. If you find it difficult, try little jogging-type runs at first, and as you progress let those runs become "small, small, *large*, small, small, *large*." Remember, you are stepping on one foot after the other:

left	right	left
small	small	large
run	run	leap

Although a leap by itself has an even rhythmic pattern, because of its greater dimension, when combined with runs, an uneven pattern results. For example:

or

4. HOP

In the hop, the takeoff into the air is from one foot and the landing is on the same foot. The hop must begin and end in demi-plié. When in the air, the leg may be straightened. The free leg has many options: it can be bent or straight, with the foot flexed or extended. The arms have various possibilities: hands on hips, arms stretched outward or upward or downward. The rhythm of a hop is even and usually rather quick. For example:

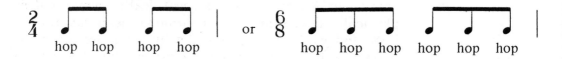

One can hop in any direction: forward, backward, circling, and so on. Hops can be shifted from one foot to another and can also be combined with other movements.

The Schottische step is a good way to practice hops in combination with runs and walks. Here is a variation:

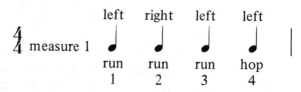

measure 2 Repeat, starting on the right foot.

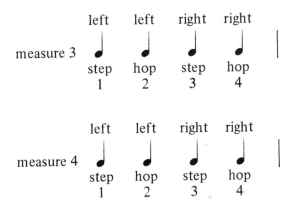

	left	left	right	right	
measure 3	♩	♩	♩	♩	│
	step	hop	step	hop	
	1	2	3	4	

	left	left	right	right	
measure 4	♩	♩	♩	♩	│
	step	hop	step	hop	
	1	2	3	4	

5. JUMP

After a slight plié, the weight is thrust into the air, taking off from both feet, extending the legs and feet while in the air, and landing on both feet. Always land on the toes and balls of the feet first, then the heels, and continue into a demi-plié. A flat-footed landing produces a teeth-shattering thud! It is possible to take off from one foot, but the landing is always on both. Jumps are done for height, to cover space, or to do interesting and expressive things while in the air. The rhythmic pattern of the jump is even:

$\frac{4}{4}$	♩	♩	♩	♩	│
	jump	jump	jump	jump	
	1	2	3	4	

Suggestions

Try jumping and turning while airborne. Fling the legs apart and together or kick the legs into a split while up in the air.

FIGURE 3-2
Split jump
Marj Cox

Think of things to do with the arms, head, and remainder of the body.

Try combinations of jumps and other movements. For example: jump, jump, walk, walk, hop, jump.

6. SKIP

A skip can also be called a step-hop, for that is what it is. The rhythm of the skip is an uneven long-short.[1]

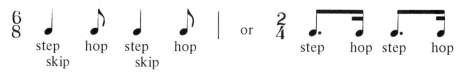

Keep the body high, swing the arms in opposition, and you will manage to attain height. Skipping gives one a sense of freedom and abandon. Perhaps that is why children often skip on their way home from school.

FIGURE 3-3
Skip
Marj Cox

Try skipping across the floor just for the enjoyment. Now try skip, skip, run, run, skip, skip, run, run. Skip forward, backward, to the side, or while turning.

[1]Some prefer to think of the skip as beginning with the upbeat (hop-step). In that case, the rhythm is an uneven short-long:

7. SLIDE

The slide has an uneven rhythmic pattern. To facilitate the beginning of a sliding pattern, start with an upbeat before the step-drag movement occurs. There is a quick weight shift or hop on the opposite foot before the step-close. If you start the slide on the left foot, that foot will remain the lead foot and the right will always be the sliding or closing foot.

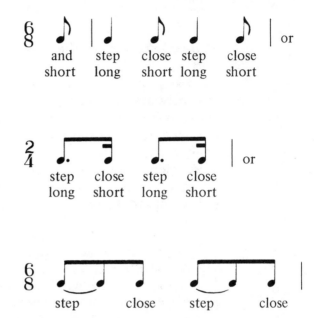

The rhythmic pattern of the slide can be analyzed differently. The one described above is not the only one, but it is one that works well. Slides are most easily done to the side while facing front, although they can be accomplished in any direction. Slides are frequently utilized in folk dances and have a buoyant, gliding quality.

Try the following:

Face your partner, both hands joined if you wish, and, starting on opposite legs, slide across the floor.

For variety, slide eight forward, four backward, eight forward, four backward.

Turn away from your partner (back to back) for every other phrase of slides.

8. GALLOP

Short-long: a gallop is a bit like having a sore foot. Walk across the floor quickly, remembering that the left foot cannot support weight more than a moment, and you will feel the rhythm of the gallop:[2]

Now make it more bouncy—perhaps to the tune of the *William Tell Overture* (the *Lone Ranger* theme). One foot will lead. The lead foot can be changed occasionally with an extra step or a pause. Usually the feet are picked up in a sprightly manner after contacting the floor. What you do with the rest of your body is entirely up to you.

Now that the basic locomotor movements have been analyzed separately, it is possible to vary or combine them. Here are two suggestions to show you how locomotor movements can be used as materials for dance. These will stimulate you to think of others.

> Observe the walks of people on campus, in your neighborhood, or downtown. Choose an interesting or unusual style of walking and learn it. Practice the walk until you are comfortable and accurate. Now exaggerate it until it becomes an abstract movement pattern. Change it in any way you wish, but be true to the theme of the original movement. Show others your rendition of the original walk and also your expanded movement pattern.
>
> Arrange the following locomotor activities in any order and continue in that order across the floor:
> - 2 walks
> - 1 skip
> - 3 slides

If each member of a class arranges his or her sequence, several interesting patterns will evolve. If the class is to perform at the same time, a steady underlying beat can serve for all.

---

[2]Sometimes the gallop is described as a step-leap and the rhythm is described as long-short:

TRIPLETS Although not generally included in listings of fundamental locomotor movements, triplets are frequently found in modern dance technique classes. They are sometimes called the waltz run or referred to unceremoniously as "down-ups."

$\frac{3}{4}$	Count	
	1	Step forward on the left foot into a demi-plié (a dance walk)
	2	Step on the right foot *en relevé*
	3	Step on the left foot *en relevé*
	1	Step forward on the right foot into demi-plié
	2	Step on the left foot *en relevé*
	3	Step on the right foot *en relevé*

Triplets are done slowly at first until the movements of the legs and the strong uplifted posture of the body are mastered. Arms can be held still at the sides or raised in second position. If preferred, the arms can swing in opposition to the legs, changing only on the first beat of each measure. When triplets are done slowly and deliberately, the emphasis is on the contrast between the plié and the relevé and the resultant change of the level of the body. As the tempo is increased, triplets can be transformed into a more flexible easy run, with the feeling of down, up, up retained but without so much emphasis on flexion and extension of the legs. Rather, the emphasis is on the flowing down-up movement of the body as it moves rapidly across the floor.

Try adding turns as follows:

$\frac{3}{4}$	Count	
	1	Moving forward, step down into plié on the left foot
	2	Relevé right
	3	Relevé left
	1	Step down into plié on right
	2	Relevé left
	3	Relevé right
	1	Step down into plié on left while turning partially to the left

2   Continue the turning movement while stepping *en relevé* right

3   Complete the turn while stepping *en relevé* left

Repeat measure three to the right, starting on the right foot. Triplets can also be performed as leap, run, run if a leap is substituted for the down movement.

AXIAL MOVEMENT

Axial movement is often described as nonlocomotor movement in that the body moves *in* space rather than *through* space. The base remains stationary, and the movement occurs around the axis of the body produced by that base. Axial movement is limited to those parts of the body not involved in the support of the body (the base).

These parts can move by flexion, extension, rotation, adduction, abduction, and circumduction, depending on anatomical limitations.

Find a base of support on which you are comfortable. "Glue" those parts of your body to the floor and then see how much movement of the rest of the body is possible. Explore all the axial movement possibilities of bending, stretching, twisting, turning, rising, falling, swinging, swaying, striking, shaking, posing, and so on.

When you have depleted the possibilities, move on to another base and repeat.

FIGURE 3-4
Axial movement
Peter Krayer

Try a third base. Perhaps the level of your body has changed or you are no longer facing in the same direction. Vary the dynamics of your movements; make some strong and others weak. Vary the flow from bound to free. Change the rhythm, focus, and style of your movements.

Work with a partner in unison, in succession, or in opposition.

You will discover that the more body parts in contact with the floor, the more stable will be your base. However, fewer parts are capable of movement, and therefore your range of movement is more limited. As your base becomes smaller, as in standing on one foot, in a handstand, or *en pointe*, balance is difficult, although the movement range is enormous.

If you are in class, look around and be sure your base is different from everyone else's.

Following are some problems to solve utilizing axial movement:

> From an appropriate base, move only isolated parts of the body, such as the head and shoulders, and explore the full range of possibilities.
>
> Axial movement exploration can be investigated by the suggestions of another person at first; later one's own ideas will flow—rise, fall, stretch sideward, spiral downward, contract, expand, collapse.
>
> Try using prepositions for movement stimulus: toward, between, among, over, under.
>
> Rhythmic accompaniment will change the character of the motion. For example, a drum beat tends to produce sudden explosive movements, a Chopin waltz most likely produces easy flowing movements, while a jazz accompaniment provokes syncopated movements. While each of us naturally relates to certain rhythmic stimuli, it is helpful to experience the unfamiliar, too, for that is when one's imagination is stretched and more unusual movements are produced.
>
> With a partner explore movement from one shape to another. Partner A strikes a pose. Partner B relates to that pose by assuming a pose which fits through some of the negative (empty) spaces created by A's pose. When B's movement reaches it conclusion, A begins a movement which takes him or her through some of the negative spaces created by B's pose, and so on.

FIGURE 3-5
Moving into negative spaces
Marj Cox

Rarely is a dance or even a movement phrase limited to locomotor or axial movements alone. They are separated here for clarity. When you walk across campus with a friend, your walk is locomotor because you need to get from chemistry lab to the English lecture hall, but your arms swing in an axial movement. And what about all those jaw movements, eye movements, and the gestures of your hands?

To bridge the gap between locomotor and axial movements, try this. Assume a shape. When it is to your liking, develop a second shape and a third. Now try different ways of moving from shape one to shape two to shape three. At first the transitions may be done in axial movements, but eventually ways of making locomotor transitions will evolve.

Combine both locomotion and nonlocomotion. Jump and clap hands. Run while slowly extending one arm over the head and reaching forward. Invent your own combination.

Here are five tasks to help you experience the contrast between locomotor and axial ways of moving:

1. Move your head and shoulders.
2. Walk to another part of the room.
3. Fall to the floor; rise.

4. Return to your original place, using any locomotor movement.

5. Move your head and one arm.

Continue the pattern until it flows and has a rhythmic feel to it.

FLOOR PATTERNS

A floor pattern is produced by locomotor movement. Visualize what would happen if you were to run around the studio after stepping in a can of paint. In actuality, the design created by locomotor movement is a fleeting one, and therefore in dance it must be carefully planned and clearly stated to enable the audience to see and remember it. Move forward, backward, to one side or the other, or in a circle. One does not always need to face forward when moving in a line of direction. To move to one side, it is possible to do so by making a quarter turn and moving forward in that direction. Or, as seventeenth-century ballet innovators discovered, by turning the legs outward it is possible to continue to face the audience while moving to the left or right. Some dance historians imply that it was thought to be impolite to turn one's face away from the audience, hence the development of the turned-out position of the legs, which has become a hallmark of the classical ballet technique.

Pathways in space can be straight or round or can also be made on the diagonal or in combinations such as zigzags, spirals, or figure eights. Try several.

These are all horizontal uses of directions in space. Because human movement is three-dimensional, one can also move vertically in combination with any of the above horizontal directions.

Try these directional problems:

From a starting position anywhere in space, explore the floor pattern of a square, a circle, a triangle, and so on. If working in a group, remember that your "personal" space, or "kinesphere," as Rudolf von Laban[3] called it, can overlap

[3]Rudolf von Laban, *Modern Educational Dance*, 2nd ed., rev. Lisa Ullmann (New York and Washington: Frederick A. Praeger, 1968).

FIGURE 3-6
Write your name by walking through space
E. Scott Lucia

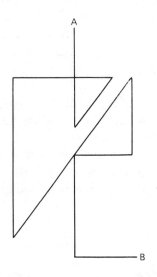

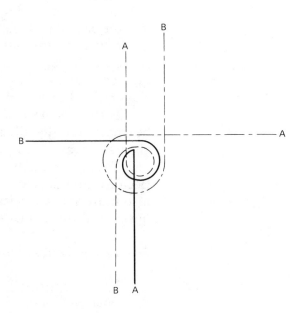

FIGURE 3-7
Design for locomotor
movement (dancer moves
from A to B)
Henry Duffy

FIGURE 3-8
Design for group locomotor movement
Henry Duffy

your neighbor's, becoming "general" space, provided that you guard against collisions. In fact, the total picture produced by intersecting floor patterns made by several individuals can indeed be an interesting one. Explore directions with different aspects of the body facing in the line of direction.

From a starting point, write your name by walking through space. Don't forget to dot the *i*'s with a jump!

With construction paper and a magic marker, draw a single-line design. Now trace the pattern on the floor, using locomotor movement. Let someone else decide whether you have been true to the design.

With a small group, a design can be drawn on paper and translated into locomotor movements. The group can move through the design in single file or in succession, or different people can begin and end at different points in the pattern.

AXIAL DESIGN (Contour or Shape)

The contour or shape made by the body moving in space around a fixed base or axis is referred to as the axial or spatial design. It is determined by several factors. The directions in which the various parts of the body can move are the same as the locomotor directions of the floor pattern: forward, backward, sideward, diagonally, circularly, upward, and downward. In fact, as one part of the

FIGURE 3-9
Axial design
Ken Roesser

body moves in one direction, other parts can move in other directions.

Suggestions:

> From the tailor sitting position, move both arms upward while the head drops and the torso leans forward.
>
> From a kneeling position, lean backward with the torso while reaching forward with the arms.

The shape or contour of the body as it cuts through space helps to define the axial design. The body contour may be straight or rounded or sharply angular. The body can appear flat, thick, thin, round, jagged, etc. Contour refers to the shape of each individual dancer. When moving in a group, the design is produced by the interaction and relationship of several individual contours.

Suggestions:

> From a fixed base, explore the directions in space, maintaining a curvilinear contour of the body.
>
> Explore all directions in space, but occasionally change the body contour.
>
> The spatial design or contour of the body is not to be ignored when in locomotion. Walk stiff-legged on tiptoes with arms stretched over head and your shape will be as straight as a pencil. Run while keeping the body rounded and the knees slightly bent and you may resemble a fast-moving egg.

Level The level in which either locomotor or axial movement is accomplished enhances spatial design. As previously mentioned, one of the differences between modern dance and ballet, often noticed, is that modern dance seems to make much use of the lowest level possible—falling to the floor, rolling, writhing, slithering about—whereas ballet is more apt to favor the highest levels. This stereotype is true to a degree, but modern dancers also like to soar through the air, and ballet dancers fall to the floor on occasion.

Explore movement on different levels as follows:

> From the lowest base, lying, move upward to sitting, crouching, kneeling, to standing, and finally to locomotion which elevates the body.

FIGURE 3-10
Movement on different levels
Marj Cox

Work with three groups, each with a leader and each group starting on one of the three levels. Follow the movement of your leader in unison. The leader must remember to keep his or her focus forward so that the gaze of the group may also focus forward in order to watch the leader at all times. Change leaders and assigned levels frequently so that many movement possibilities can be explored by all. The three leaders may relate to each other and change levels occasionally, ever mindful of the need to keep one group on each level. If the group which started on a high level appears to be preparing to fall to the floor, the group which has been exploring the low level might prepare to rise to a high level. These shifts can be made without preplanning or verbal communication.

The following problem utilizes axial and locomotor movement:

Study carefully your favorite sculpture. Learn to place your body in the shape of the sculpture. You may need to bring a photograph or sketch to the studio if your visual memory is not dependable. Begin in the contour of the sculpture. Explore the axial movement possibilities from your base. Perhaps you would like to change the base to that of another level and explore new movement possibilities from a new level, keeping the character of the original in mind. Experiment with locomotor movement as well as axial movement, ever mindful of the original design. Move the way that sculpture might move if suddenly given mobility. Return to the original shape.

FIGURE 3-12
Movement from the pose
Ken Roesser

FIGURE 3-11
Pose inspired by Picasso's *Woman with Apple,*
1943
Ken Roesser

In Figure 3–11 the dancer's pose is inspired by Picasso's *Woman with Apple.* Figure 3–12 shows the beginning of movement from that pose.

Your favorite painting or photograph will also serve as a starting point for an interesting movement study. Begin in the poses of the people in the chosen picture. Then move in ways which you think would be appropriate. Complete the study by returning to the original pose.

Walt Kuhn's *Trio* provides three dancers with a pose from which to explore movement.

FIGURE 3-13
Walt Kuhn's *Trio* (1937)
Colorado Springs Fine Arts Center, Gift
of the El Pomar Foundation.
Used with permission.

FIGURE 3-14
Three dancers in pose
Marj Cox

FIGURE 3-15
Dancers moving from the pose
Marj Cox

Focus of the eyes is important in dance in two ways. First, balance is enhanced when the eyes are focused on a stationary point. Stand on one foot, rise to half toe, and experience the difference in balancing when you watch moving bodies in front of you or when you focus on that spot on the wall. When in motion, such as when walking across a balance beam or a railroad track, you will find that focus of the eyes keeps you on a steady keel.

In turning or spinning consecutively, one must learn to "spot," or one loses one's balance and dizziness results. When spotting, a dancer focuses on a point in front, and as the body turns the eyes remain fixed on that spot as long as possible. As the body rotates, the head turns quickly and the eyes return to the original spot.

Second, the communicative aspect of dance is given emphasis when movement is punctuated by focus. Stand on a busy city street corner and look upward. Before long, passers-by will also steal a glance in the same direction. Or watch the heads of the spectators at a tennis match and you will know where the ball is, when the point is won, and who fumbled the return.

Focus must be considered in all dance movement. It gives direction and meaning to movement. It is not always

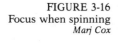
FIGURE 3-16
Focus when spinning
Marj Cox

necessary to focus the eyes in the line of direction. In fact, a greater impact is sometimes achieved when the focus is not in the same direction as that in which the body is moving.

Try this:

> Focus on a point in the studio such as a clock. Without losing eye contact with that clock, explore all movements in relation to it. Now switch to a crack in the floor, the ceiling, someone else's back, or your own big toe. The character of your improvisational movement gains clarity and purpose as you concentrate and focus on a single point.

Or, try the reverse:

> Invent a movement phrase with a definite focus. Now change that focus to another point in space for the entire phrase of movement. Or, change the focus more than once during the execution of the phrase. Notice how the movement appears to be altered by the focal changes.

Your audience, too, will find meaning in your dance if it senses the intensity of your conscious point of focus. Beginners in dance appear to be more polished even in simple class studies when focus is directed rather than random. When performing, focus helps to project to the audience the intensity and intent of the dancer.

Dimension (Range or Amplitude)

Dimension refers to the size of a movement or to the amount of space covered by the movement. Body motion ranges from small to large. Find the smallest movement you are capable of, such as a blink of the eyelid or a flick of the little finger. Progressively increase the range of your tiny motion. The little-finger flick expands to include the whole hand, the arm, the entire body, and finally bursts into locomotion through space. Gradually diminish the dimension until you return to a minute flick of one little finger. When working with a group, the dimensional effect can also be enlarged or diminished by the addition or subtraction of a number of dancers.

Dimension is also related to the level and direction of the body as it moves in space: how high, how wide, and how deep is the motion? Dimension also defines the plane of the movement, whether it is vertical, horizontal or diagonal.

Try this dimension problem:

> Develop a locomotor movement pattern, such as four skips, two runs, and a walk. Count the number of times the pattern must be done in order to cover a given amount of space. Can the same amount of space be covered if the dimension of the movement pattern is increased or decreased?

Summary Utilizing all of the spatial information you have learned, create a three-part movement study.

Part A:

Imagine yourself within the confines of a specific shape: a box such as one which carries a dozen long-stemmed red roses, a balloon, a sardine can, or the sections of a revolving door. Outline with your movements all perimeters of the chosen shape. In doing so, utilize locomotor or axial movement as appropriate. Think of directions, levels, focus, and dimension. Do not pantomine, but instead keep your movements exaggerated and abstract. When you feel that you have adequately communicated the size and shape of your container, part A is completed.

Part B:

If you were within that container, how would you attempt to escape? Can you lift off a lid and then climb over the side? Can you break through the walls by punching and kicking? Is it possible to crawl or roll under a part of your confinement? In exploring the possibilities of escape, you will communicate more information about the size and shape of your chosen container.

Part C or A:

The third part of this study depends on the degree of success achieved in part B. If you succeeded in escaping, you will so indicate by moving away from the originally designated floor pattern or spatial design and by taking advantage of this new-found freedom in any way you wish.

This part is then designated C, and the dance study can be described as being in ABC form. If, on the other hand, the boundaries were too vast, too high, or impermeable, and if after adequate investigation you must resign yourself to remaining within the designated container, communicate this fact by returning to the original part A and continue exploration of the space involved, in which case you have designed a movement pattern with an ABA form. The above problem can be an interesting one for groups to solve. In a class situation, when groups of four or five people show their studies to the others in the class, their skill in communication is tested by the readiness displayed by the audience in determining the shape of the container used.

In summary, it is important to note that factors influencing the use of space which have been considered are all interdependent and are influenced by, and will influence, the following analyses of the factors of time and force. Keep them in mind as you continue to study the remainder of this chapter, and the relationships which contribute to the totality of body motion will become evident.

TIME All motion as well as stillness occurs in time. Dance utilizes time in ways that determine the rhythm, tempo, and duration of movements. When we consider time, we turn our attention to that rather difficult-to-define term, rhythm, which has been described as the flow of movement or the regular recurrence of beats. There are natural rhythms of the human body, such as the rhythm of the heartbeat and the breath; there are externally imposed rhythms in our environment, such as that of the ticking clock, and there is the metric rhythm of music. Rhythm occurs in all art forms. Dance can relate to the rhythm of any other art, but the most common relationship throughout history has been with music. The dancer therefore, must understand metric rhythm.

Metric Rhythm Metric rhythm results from the grouping and pattern of accents, beats, and pulses. The signature found at the beginning of a piece of music gives information about the temporal values of the notes which follow and determines where the measure markers fall. Accents generally occur on the first beat of a measure in traditional music, and therefore one can learn to count measures when listening to the fall of accents.

The relationship of one note to another is a mathematically logical binary division. When a quarter note is assigned one beat ($\quarternote = 1$), the relationship diagramed below exists:

whole note $\mathbf{o}$ = 4 counts

half note $\halfnote$ = 2 counts

quarter note $\quarternote$ = 1 count

eighth note $\eighthnote$ = ½ count

sixteenth note $\sixteenthnote$ = ¼ count

The above relationship occurs whenever the denominator of the time signature[4] is 4, indicating that a quarter note is equal to one beat, as in $\frac{4}{4}, \frac{2}{4}, \frac{3}{4}, \frac{5}{4},$ and so on. If, however, the denominator of the time signature is 8, as in $\frac{6}{8}$ time, an eighth note has one beat. Then the comparable values of all the notes are as follows:

$$\frac{6}{8}$$

half note $\halfnote$ = 4

quarter note $\quarternote$ = 2

eighth note $\eighthnote$ = 1

sixteenth note $\sixteenthnote$ = ½

The numerator of the time signature simply states the number of beats per measure. A measure consists of the notes and rests which fall between the bars. For example:

[4]The time signature is sometimes called the meter signature or musical signature.

4 there are 4 beats per measure
4 a quarter note equals 1 beat

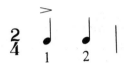

6 there are 6 beats per measure
8 an eighth note equals 1 beat

Tertiary division occurs, as in triplets, when three notes assume the value of one beat:

One can learn these relationships of one note to another kinesthetically by clapping, walking, or playing percussion instruments. For example in $\frac{4}{4}$ time, a drum beat can be used to signify the quarter note. Keeping a steady moderate rhythm, think of the quarter note as the underlying beat.

Now play the finger cymbals so that the sound is sustained twice as long for the half note.

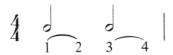

The gong serves as an excellent example of the whole note.

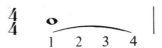

Let us return to our underlying beat, the quarter note with the drum, for a moment, and then move along to the quicker notes. Castanets can be used to play the eighth notes.

Now shake the maraca to demonstrate the sixteenth notes.

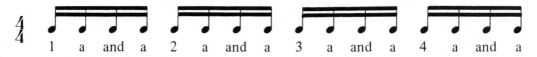

If working with a group of five or more people, assign one of each of the five instruments to one person, and have everyone play them in unison. The person playing the drum sets the tempo of the underlying beat, and all the others must coincide. If there are enough people, designate some as musicians and the others as dancers. Each dancer moves in time with the note value of the musician he or she is working with. Movement patterns can be developed that correspond to each note value. The rhythm band could play as directed:

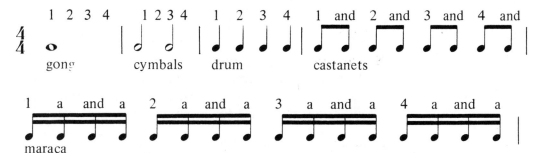

or all musicians could play simultaneously, ever mindful of the underlying beat.

RESTS AND DOTS

When reading music, a dancer must also understand the metric value of rests which often appear within a measure.

whole rest	▬	=	𝅝
half rest	▬	=	𝅗𝅥
quarter rest	𝄽	=	♩
eighth rest	𝄾	=	♪
sixteenth rest	𝄿	=	𝅘𝅥𝅯

When a dot follows a note, the dot assigns to that note one half in addition to its usual value. For example:

𝅝· = 6 beats

𝅗𝅥· = 3 beats

♩· = 1 1/2 beats

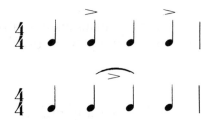

♪. = 3/4 beat

♪. = 3/8 beat

Syncopation occurs when the accent falls on normally weaker beats, producing an irregular rhythm. Sometimes the accent occurs on a normally weaker beat and is extended to or beyond the normally accented beat.

Examples:

EVEN AND UNEVEN RHYTHMS

In the discussion of time signatures, we saw how even rhythmic patterns are produced in music. When all the notes in a measure are of equal value, an even pattern results.

$\frac{3}{4}$ ♩ ♩ ♩ | ♩ ♩ ♩ | ♩ ♩ ♩ | ♩ ♩ ♩ |
  1 2 3   1 2 3   1 2 3   1 2 3

This is called primary rhythm and establishes the fundamental or underlying beat (or pulse).

    Conversely, when all the notes within a measure are not of equal value, an uneven rhythmic pattern results. This is referred to as the secondary rhythm and corresponds to the melody in music.

Suggestions:

The two examples above use the same time signature, the same number of measures, and the same tempo.

Clap each example.

Create a movement pattern for each. Movements with even rhythmic patterns are often simple, balanced, and restful, sometimes even boring. Movements with uneven rhythmic patterns can be exciting, unusual, more demanding. Usually our movements alternate between even and uneven rhythms.

Perhaps you remember that five of the eight basic locomotor movements have even rhythmic patterns—walk, run, leap, hop, and jump—while skip, gallop, and slide produce uneven rhythmic patterns. However, if more than one of the even locomotor movements are combined, an uneven rhythm often results. Run-run-leap (short-short-long) is a prime example.

If the tempo of the same movement is varied, an uneven rhythm can be produced.

For example:

walk slowly—walk slowly—walk quickly 3 times
   long   long   short short short

Any name, phrase, or sentence can be analyzed for its rhythmic pattern and translated into movement. Consider several.

Environmental sounds, such as the chirp of the cicada or the fall of rain on the roof, sometimes produce even and sometimes uneven rhythmic patterns. These can serve as accompaniment for movement patterns.

Tempo

Tempo is the rate of speed at which one moves. In music, tempo is not dependent on the time signature but instead receives its instructions from terminology found at the beginning of a section of music and can be regulated by the metronome.

For example:

lento or largo   slow, heavy
adagio   slow and stately

moderato or andante	moderate
allegro	quick and spritely
presto	very fast

Compare these tempos to the note values previously learned, and move accordingly.

When dancing with a musical accompaniment, one may adhere to the tempo of the music, sometimes reacting to the fundamental beat, or one may move twice as fast or twice as slowly, or in any other relevant rhythmic manner.

For example, with a partner who beats or claps a steady rhythm, experiment with moving to the beat. Now try moving twice as fast or four times as fast, and so on.

With a partner, move across the floor, stepping on every beat:

while your partner moves twice as fast:

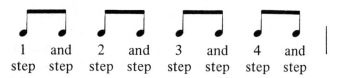

1	and	2	and	3	and	4	and
step	step	step	step	step	step	step	step

Now reverse patterns for the second measure. Your floor patterns will be one of moving ahead and catching up, for as we learned when exploring space, when one progresses with eight runs instead of four walks, a greater use of space is evident. Thus when the tempo increases, the dimension of the space used also increases.

Tempo does not always remain constant. Sometimes tempo accelerates or decelerates (retards). Usually, as the tempo of one's movements accelerates markedly, there is a corresponding increase in the dimension of the floor space covered, but often each individual movement becomes progressively smaller.

For example, swing your arm forward to shoulder height, down to the side of your body, and out to the side at shoulder height, using an even rhythm. Gradually accelerate the tempo of the pendulous movement until the dimension of the movement must decrease to accomplish one pendulum for each beat. However, when walking across the floor next to a partner, the person who steps slowly does not arrive at the end of the room as soon as does the one who steps more quickly with many steps, each of which is of smaller dimension.

When we speak of tempo, we are referring to a relative situation. A movement may be faster than another one, or slower, or four times faster, or faster at first and then slower than something else.

TEMPO PROBLEM

If you have a hula hoop, try this. Hold the hula hoop on end. Spin it, let go, and watch how the tempo of the hoop's movements increases as the hoop falls toward the floor and the dimension of space used decreases. As you watch the hoop fall to its final stillness on the floor, create a movement pattern which follows the tempo and dimension of the hoop's motion. A similar situation exists when a ball is bounced once and let go. Each successive bounce will be smaller and quicker. The ball can also serve as a stimulus for a movement pattern.

Phrase A phrase is a group of measures of music or a series of rhythmic impulses or movements in dance. A phrase expresses a partially completed idea. Many phrases are joined together to form a section of a dance or of a piece of music. If you have danced the Virginia Reel, for example, you have experienced movement phrases: "Everbody forward and back," "Dos-à-dos with your partner," and so on.

When creating movement without musical accompaniment, one is free to make a phrase of movement of any length. Often within a dance section, phrases are of the same length, but this is, of course, not necessary.

Create a movement phrase. Repeat it until you have learned it well. Then think of some of the interesting ways the phrase can be varied.

For example:

Repeat the phrase on a different level. Perform the phrase twice as fast. If a locomotor phrase, change the direction in space or change the level.

Duration Duration refers to the length of time expended by a movement. Duration can be measured; it can be regulated by an externally imposed force such as a drum beat or musical accompaniment, by a clock or stop watch, or by the dancer's own sense of timing. Dancers often refer to movements as long or short.

Suggestions:

> Using a steady beat of eight counts, perform a simple movement, such as a flexion and extension of a particular body part. Now repeat the same movement twice within the eight counts. Next repeat the movement four times within the duration of the eight counts. Now return to the original statement of movement done to eight counts. You have witnessed an example of how duration of movement affects the tempo as well as the use of space. For when the duration of time remained the same and the motions were doubled and quadrupled, the tempo of one's movements were increased. The dimensions of space utilized correspondingly diminished.

To test one's innate sense of time, create a movement pattern which takes eight seconds to perform. Can you learn to perform it each time within eight seconds: Can you perform it twice as fast so that it is completed twice in eight seconds? What about three times? Or, perform it twice as slowly in sixteen seconds.

When the duration of a movement pattern changes, notice how the quality of the movement is affected and also the use of space.

Duration refers not only to the time in which a movement occurs, but also the length of time of a dance, a group of dances, or of a performance.

Rhythmic Devices The employment of various rhythmic devices helps musicians and dancers to achieve variety in composition. You will enjoy experimenting with some of them which follow.

ACCUMULATIVE AND DECUMULATIVE METER

Accumulative or cumulative meter occurs when each measure of a piece of music is written in a different meter and there is a regular increase of beats per measure. For example:

or

Decumulative or diminishing meter occurs when the reverse situation exists. For example:

C. (musical notation)

Accumulative and decumulative meter can be used in combination, as follows:

97

Create a movement using the rhythmic structure of example A. Adapt the movement pattern so that it can be repeated to the rhythmic structure of example C. Combine the two parts utilizing example D. For instance, using a simple walking pattern, change direction on the accented first beat of each measure.

MIXED METER

Mixed meter is found most often in contemporary music and is a device useful for creating interest and surprise. Any arrangement of time signatures is possible, for example:

COUNTERPOINT

In music, counterpoint consists of combining two or more melodies simultaneously. In dance, two or more dancers can produce the same effect when moving simultaneously in contrasting but harmonious movement.

RESULTANT RHYTHM

Resultant rhythm is a form of polymeter. When the rhythmic pattern produced by the accents of a given number of measures of a specific time signature is superimposed on the same number of beats, governed by a different time signature, the rhythm which results from the accents of both phrases is called the resultant rhythm.

For example:

$\frac{4}{4}$ | $\overset{>}{1}$ 2 3 4 | $\overset{>}{2}$ 2 3 4 | $\overset{>}{3}$ 2 3 4 | The accents which occur in 3 measures of $\frac{4}{4}$

$\frac{3}{4}$ | $\overset{>}{1}$ 2 3 | $\overset{>}{2}$ 2 3 | $\overset{>}{3}$ 2 3 | $\overset{>}{4}$ 2 3 | plus 4 measures of $\frac{3}{4}$ equals

$\frac{12}{4}$ | $\overset{>}{1}$ 2 3 $\overset{>}{4}$ $\overset{>}{5}$ 6 $\overset{>}{7}$ 8 $\overset{>}{9}$ $\overset{>}{10}$ 11 12 | 1 measure of $\frac{12}{4}$

Clap each phrase, accenting the first beat of each of the $\frac{4}{4}$ and $\frac{3}{4}$ measures. Learn the accents of the $\frac{12}{4}$ measure by listening to two people or two groups clapping the $\frac{3}{4}$ and the $\frac{4}{4}$ phrases simultaneously. Develop a movement phrase which utilizes the accents described above for the three measures of $\frac{4}{4}$ time, a phrase utilizing the accents of the four measures of $\frac{3}{4}$ time, and a phrase utilizing the accents produced by the resultant rhythm.

If working with a group of three or more people, divide the group into three smaller groups and create a dance study with the following form. Group A creates a movement phrase which corresponds to the $\frac{4}{4}$ segment. Group B creates a movement phrase which corresponds to the $\frac{3}{4}$ segment. Group C creates a movement phrase of one measure of $\frac{12}{4}$ with accented movement on counts 1, 4, 5, 7, 9, and 10.

After each group shows its patterns to the others, the groups can be arranged according to the directions and dimensions of space utilized.

Now perform the parts of the study as a unit, as follows:

Group A	12 counts
Group B	12 counts
Group C	12 counts
Groups A, B, C	12 counts in unison

Resultant rhythm can also be achieved by superimposing three rhythmic patterns.

TIME PROBLEM

Test your understanding of rhythm by solving the following problem. Write a short piece of music using any time signature and any rhythmic device desired. Only the rhythmic pattern of the music is necessary, for we are not concerned with melody. The rhythmic pattern can be clapped, played by percussion instruments, or "sung" by voice sounds.

Compose a movement pattern which corresponds rhythmically to the rhythmic pattern. Consider all aspects of space previously learned. Perform the piece with accompaniment, if possible.

Nonmetric Rhythms   The rhythm of spoken words, of environmental sounds, of electronic music, or of the heartbeat are also suitable for dance accompaniment. Explore these possibilities with improvisational movement and create movement phrases to the accompaniment of nonmetric rhythms. The results will be interesting. Dancers need not always be dependent on music. Some dancers have even created dances with no sound accompaniment. The audience's attention is concentrated on movement patterns and spatial awareness, undiluted by auditory stimuli. Some members of the audience are not ready for this, for it is challenging.

FORCE   You have explored the uses of space, you have experimented with time in its many variations, and you have seen how space and time are influenced by one another and are, therefore, interdependent. Although you have not been conscious of force (and energy), it is always present when motion occurs.

Dynamics   Dynamics is the force of movement. Every movement against gravity requires force in varying amounts, but the same movement can be made with a minimum of force or with great power. The dynamics of movement results from the amount of force expended and the ways in which control is exerted. It is through these subtleties of dynamics that contrasts are produced in the quality of movement. Because these variations in effort produced by the dancer aid in communication to an audience, they are worthy of analysis and study. Here are five movement qualities to be considered.

FIGURE 3-17
Percussive movement
Peter Krayer

QUALITIES OF MOVEMENT

PERCUSSIVE MOVEMENT   Percussive movements are sharp, explosive, and often aggressive. The energy is applied with a sudden outburst and is stopped immediately. There is no follow through. Percussive movement can be compared to a staccato note on the piano or to hitting a nail with a hammer or, in fact, to any striking or kicking movement. Find a partner. If you do not have one, work with an imaginary one. Pretend that you and your partner are boxing, fencing, or chopping wood. On count 1, you strike, and your partner will recoil; on count 2, reverse your roles. Be sure to remember the counts so there are no collisions! Percussive movements, you will discover, are extremely vigorous and require a great deal of energy. the larger the movement, the more quickly and strongly the energy must be expended. The moods which are communicated are outward, aggressive, and strong, such as anger.

SUSTAINED MOVEMENT   Sustained movement is accomplished when the energy is released in a smooth, strong, continuous manner with a high degree of control throughout the movement. The sense of control emanates from the center of the body, and there is no letting go of energy until the movement is complete. To experience

FIGURE 3-18
Sustained movement
Peter Krayer

sustained movement, imagine a cinder block on the floor in front of you. Bend down and slowly and carefully lift the cinder block high above your head. When you can lift it no higher, the sustained movement is completed. Or, try pushing a car which is stuck in the mud or moving a grand piano. Sustained movements communicate strong, often introverted and serious emotions, certainly not flighty or superficial moods.

SWINGING MOVEMENT In swinging movements, the force of energy is applied at the beginning of a movement as a small impetus to an uncontrolled follow-through which results in a relaxed movement; after this there is a pause, and either gravity takes over to complete the swinging motion, or another small impetus is needed. Swinging movements of the body can be compared to what happens when pushing a child on a swing. The push serves as the impetus, the child and the swing reach the highest point on their own, and then gravity returns the child and swing to the starting place. Another burst of energy on the part of the person pushing the swing is now required in order to continue the movement; otherwise, each successive arc will be smaller until the motion stops.

FIGURE 3-19
Swinging movement
Peter Krayer

Swinging is a natural movement. In mood it implies freedom and abandon. Some joints of the body are most inclined to swinging movements. Try several. You will find it easy to swing the arms and legs. Can you accomplish free-swinging movements in other parts of the body? Try two-beat swings, three-beat swings, and so on. Your audience will capture your mood of freedom.

VIBRATORY MOVEMENT Vibratory movements occur when there is a quick succession of many small percussive movements with little space and time between them. The energy, as with all percussive movement, is emitted quickly and suddenly and with no follow-through. The result is movement which quivers, shakes, or pulsates. The feeling generated is of fear, trepidation, or excitement.

Experiment with vibratory movements of various parts of the body. Most people will be more successful at first with small segments of the body. Watch a skilled Middle Eastern belly dancer for a clear example of vibratory movements.

COLLAPSING MOVEMENT Collapsing movement occurs when there is a release of tension of the muscles and

FIGURE 3-20
Collapsing movement
Peter Krayer

gravity takes over. This relaxation may be achieved with one or many parts of the body. Of course, one never completely collapses unless one is unconscious, but when many parts of the body are relaxed and only those muscles which are necessary for control and safety are contracted, a collapsed look can be achieved. Try a Raggedy Ann or Andy–type collapse: in order, collapse the head, shoulders, arms, back, hips, knees, ankles, and finally, the entire body. Or, try to "die" like a television cowboy. The shot is fired, and it requires at least six counts before the victim finally "hits the dust." Collapse to the floor in four counts, two counts, or even one, if you are brave. Remember when falling to the floor that one must always avoid landing on the knees, the elbows, the base of the spine, and of course, the head.

We have considered five contrasting ways of releasing and controlling energy, and the resultant qualities have enabled us to communicate vastly different moods.

A dancer does not necessarily limit his or her range of movement quality to just one—this would result in monotony—unless the dancer wishes to make a dynamic statement by doing so. Often one part of the body is releasing energy in one manner while another group of muscles is doing so in a different way. Consider a simple walk that you do while chatting with a friend. The legs may be moving in a sustained manner, the arms are swinging or gesticulating percussively, and perhaps the jaw is nearly vibrating.

Dynamics problems:

> To understand the communicative possibilities of various movement qualities, let us use them in a literal way. The situation is as follows: You have just graduated from college, cum laude. You are free from studying, examinations, and all the stresses of college life. React to this freedom in swinging movements. The letter carrier is coming up the hill carrying a load of replies to all those résumés you sent out in the hope of finding a position worthy of your talents. Feel the sustained movement of the tired letter carrier as he or she slowly approaches with a heavy burden. As you prepare to open these letters, experience the vibratory movements which signify your tense anxiety. Letter after letter is negative. The tension mounts and turns from anticipation to anger. Your movements increase in time, space, and dynamics and become percussive. How can we end this scenario? The voice on the telephone which you have just answered tells you that you have won the lottery and are now a millionaire! You have guessed it: Collapse!

> Create a movement study using one of the following objects as a motivating device to establish the dynamics of the movement: a feather, a chiffon scarf, or a bean bag. The object can be tossed into the air and observed as it falls to the floor. If three people or three groups relate to one of the three, interesting contrasts will be observed.

Balance   Balance has two different meanings in dance. One is whether or not the dancer is in balance physically. Means to achieve stability, whether in a stationary pose, such as *en relevé*, or in motion, such as walking a tightrope, are as follows. First, the broader the base, the more stability. This is why one stands in a solid stride stance when riding the subway or when anticipating an opponent's moves in karate. Second, the lower the center of gravity, the more stable one is. It is a little like those dolls with the weighted bases which can be pushed in any direction and always right themselves. That is also why we are more stable when lying or sitting than when standing or *en pointe.*

Third, focus is essential. Focus on a stationary object. If you are in class, try not to look at other students in front of you or at the instructor who is in motion. Fix your eyes on a spot on the wall straight ahead, and you will find your balance. Fourth, relationship of body parts helps to create stability or lack of it. When we walk we use our arms in opposition to our legs. This is a balanced way of moving. The arms of the aerial artist are extended even beyond reach by the long pole he or she carries. Fifth, constant motion helps to maintain stability better than rigidity. This, of course, is sometimes impractical if the choreography calls for a held pose.

The dancer takes these factors into account. The audience can be fooled to think that the dancer is stable even when he or she is not by the arrangement of body parts. Or, the audience may think that the dancer is out of control when he or she is indeed simply suspended. When falling in dance, apparent loss of balance is nonetheless a controlled movement. The dancer defies gravity. He or she falls but maintains control in order to rise again.

The second consideration of balance relates to choreography. If a movement is symmetrical, it is said to be balanced; if a movement is asymmetrical, a less stable feeling is expressed. This applies to the movements of a solo dancer or to the movements of more than one dancer. The arrangement of the group can be symmetrical or asymmetrical. Each arrangement has its dynamic effect.

Explore your range of balance and loss of balance. Begin in a stable pose and move to an unbalanced position. See how far you can go before losing balance. Do the above factors help to maintain stability longer?

Experiment with balanced positions and movements. Use the mirror to see when your position is symmetrical and when it is not.

Improvise with your partner, using unison and non-unison movement. Move from balanced to unbalanced poses. Does your partner help you to be balanced at times? Or can he or she increase the possibilities for instability?

Accent An accent or stress in movement occurs when there is a change in the dynamics of movement. An accent can be a stronger movement, lack of movement, change of direc-

FIGURE 3-21
Symetrical arrangement of the group
Marj Cox

FIGURE 3-22
Asymetrical arrangement of the group
Peter Krayer

FIGURE 3-23
Balanced position
Peter Krayer

FIGURE 3-24
From a stable to an unbalanced position
Peter Krayer

FIGURE 3-25
With a partner, from balanced to unbalanced poses
Peter Krayer

FIGURE 3-26
Accent
Marj Cox

tion, level, or any of many other possibilities. The most common accent is produced by an increase of intensity, but whenever attention is called to a specific point in the movement, an accent occurs. In traditional music, we often hear the accent on count 1 of a measure. This orderly repetition of accents helps us to learn to dance "to the music," as, for example, in a waltz:

If you wish to determine the meter of a piece of music aurally, it helps to respond in movement as you listen and try to count beats. A tap of the foot or a nod of the head will soon help to determine the placement of the accents. When accenting a movement pattern, one can also do it in an auditory manner. Clap on count 1 of each measure. This produces a strong, stable, perhaps potentially monotonous pattern. Now make these accents movement accents. Arms thrust over the head on count 1, and at the sides on 2, 3, and 4.

A visual pattern is produced similar to the auditory one. If you do not wish to give your audience so much security, try the following:

Using measures of $\frac{4}{4}$ time, accent count 1 each time by turning sharply to the right. This will change the aspect of the body which faces the audience each measure.

Using four measures in $\frac{4}{4}$ time, accent the first beat of the first measure, the second beat of the second measure, and so on. This is called consecutive or progressive accent. An exciting rhythmic pattern develops.

Variable accents in which there is no regular arrangement also provide rhythmic excitement.

If you wish to communicate calmness and security, a regular pattern of accents is in order. If, on the other hand, your goal is to startle, vary the placement of accents as well as the kind.

SUMMARY You have analyzed and experimented with the components of space, time, and force. They have been considered separately, but they are in effect inseparable elements of all movement. When one component is intentionally altered for dramatic effect in dance, others will also be affected. A few examples of these interactions will help you to think about others.

When the dimension of a movement is increased, there is a corresponding increase in the amount of space used and also in the duration needed for the movement. The reverse is also true. When the tempo of a movement increases, the dimension of the movement and the amount of space used usually decrease and vice versa. We have also seen how tempo affects the quality of movement. Rapid movement produces a vibratory quality, while slow movements often become sustained.

Tempo and balance are also interrelated in that balance is sometimes more difficult during slow motion. But in certain kinds of rapid motion, great control of balance is also needed.

Space, time, and force—the inseparable three! Explore, manipulate, increase, decrease, diminish, augment, combine the components of each. Through improvisation in movement you will learn the ways in which one aspect of movement relates to another, and ultimately you will understand how to communicate thoughts, ideas, and images, through movement. This is the essence of dance.

Try the following movement study, which combines some of the elements of space, time, and force.[5]

1. Make an interesting shape with the body.
2. Make another shape on a different level.
3. Now assume another shape on a third level. The above transitions are done smoothly with sustained movements.
4. Quickly make three sudden sharp directional changes of the body, with a strong focus on each. These changes are percussive, strong, and quick.
5. Now travel around the room, using any or all locomotor movements, moving quickly and energetically, with many sharp vertical and horizontal directional changes.
6. Suddenly freeze.
7. Fall slowly in a spiraling sustained movement to the floor.

Chapter 4 offers additional suggestions for ways to initiate improvisation in dance.

[5]Adapted from a lecture-demonstration by Dee Winterton, AAHPERD Convention, Boston, April 1981.

4

IMPROVISATION

Improvisation in dance is spontaneous action that occurs without preplanning and is not necessarily remembered or repeated. It is a marvelous device for helping a dancer become comfortable in motion. Improvisational experiences help one to explore movement possibilities, to increase the range of one's movement, to discover spatial, dynamic, and rhythmic options, and to increase one's vocabulary of movement. Just as the baby makes nonsensical sounds before his or her first words are learned, the dancer must experience movement before his or her first structured dance movements are formed.

Anyone can improvise in movement; some people are more uninhibited and therefore are free to plunge in without thought and let their movements flow. For the more inhibited, motivational devices are necessary. Some like to "move to music," some must have a reason, such as transporting oneself "from here to there." While improvising one learns about the movement range of one's body: how the various parts of the body can move, how high one can jump, how fast one can run, and how slowly one can fall to the floor. One should avoid using exercises and patterns which have been learned in technique class. Also avoid copying the teacher or another student's movements.

Students who have "grown up" with the movement-education approach to learning movement skills rather than the traditional approach in physical education classes are at ease with the exploration of movement. Modern dance is the next step, and they are ready.

Highly trained dancers from structured disciplines like classical ballet often find creative movement awkward and difficult at first. Their trained bodies are accustomed to defined patterns and positions and will naturally return to these. The flow from one movement to another is often easier for a beginner than it is for a highly trained technician. Do not despair, the training pays off in other ways. Once the freedom is discovered, the body has the strength, balance, coordination, and all the attributes necessary for developing interesting movement patterns. Creativity is important, but without a tuned instrument the result is not meaningful. That is why a modern dancer must work constantly to train his or her body to increase its "motional" range and at the same time explore the endless possibilities for creative expression through movement.

Dancers who improvise before a mirror will learn much from watching movements evolve. Do not let this inhibit you, however. You will not always like what you see, but the image can be erased as soon as you move. Remember, in movement exploration there is no right or wrong, only new and different versus hackneyed and old!

Although improvisation is a process, a step, in learning to use the body as a creative expressive instrument, it can also become a device for choreography. Composition is often derived from improvisation. Some groups even use "planned improvisations" as concert pieces.

One can think of nearly endless numbers of motivational devices to stimulate improvisational movement. In the beginning, it is not wise to put on a record and attempt to "just move." The result could be a "tongue-tied" body! Beware of a teacher who improvises in front of the class; this may stimulate the others to move, but sometimes the result is thirty carbon copies of the teacher's movements— perhaps a creative experience for the teacher, but certainly for no one else! Beginners often find small tasks helpful at first. Here are a few suggestions; see Chapter 3 for additional problem-solving situations which relate to specific aspects of space, time, and force.

SUGGESTIONS FOR IMPROVISATION

ISOLATING BODY PARTS

Move only the fingers of your left hand in all possible ways: bend, stretch, rotate, shake, clench your fist, point, trace, and explore shapes the hand can make. Add the right hand. Let the hands interact. Relate to the hands of another person. Add your arms, or work with hands and other body parts. Let your hands instigate the movement and resulting shapes of other parts of the body. Finally, allow the hands to lead the rest of the body in axial and locomotor movement. Now try moving without the use of hands and arms.

WORKING WITH A PROP

Relate to a chair or other functional object. Sit on it. Crawl over it and under it, go around it, away from it, toward it, and so on. Other props, such as smooth rock, a piece of elastic, or a jagged-edged Christmas tree ornament, lend textures which stimulate movement ideas. Brooms can be utilized to enhance the line of the dancers' movements. The tactile effect is sometimes enhanced when the object is handled with closed eyes.

FIGURE 4-1
Relating to a prop
Ken Roesser

FIGURE 4-2
Brooms enhance the
lines
of the dancers'
movements
Ken Roesser

114

If the shape of the object changes in motion, such as the long ribbon used by modern rhythmic gymnasts, a different kind of challenge is posed.

Later when one is more experienced, the prop can be an imaginary one such as a mountain, a pile of leaves, or a stone wall.

RESPONDING TO IMAGERY

This is similar to moving with props, but props are actually present and are physically available to move around, over, or through, whereas a photograph of the George Washington Bridge or a memory of the Adirondack Mountains may also evoke movement response.

Imagining that one is an object such as a blender or a cuckoo clock will stimulate mechanical-type movements. Groups will enjoy putting together complex imaginary machinery, each dancer representing a gear or a piston. One must be cautioned to keep the movement abstract, not pantomimic.

RESPONDING TO WORDS

Words suggested by another person will instigate movement responses: drop, climb, collapse, roll, bounce, stretch, bend, slash, clamor, dissolve. Or, the dancer can speak and respond in movement to words or to onomatopoetic words such as whoops, boom, shshsh.

Poetry or prose can serve the more experienced improviser. It is also possible to move in response to a reader. For example, T.S. Eliot's "The Hollow Men" or the thirteenth chapter of First Corinthians. Again, try to avoid using pantomime, for that is a different medium of expression.

RESPONDING TO SOUNDS

Listen and respond to sounds such as the bouncing of a ball, the shaking of a rattle, the ticking of a clock or a metronome. Environmental sounds such as a thunderstorm, a sledge hammer, the steady drip of a faucet, when recorded, can serve as movement stimuli. Recordings of environmental sounds can be purchased, or you can tape your own. Vocal or body sounds of the dancer can also instigate movement. Try a cough, sneeze, hiccough. Also clap, stamp, scratch, and so on.

While this seems to be the most logical way to stimulate improvisation, it has been a stumbling block for many. It is not sufficient to turn on the music and dance; you must first decide how the music is going to be used. Are you going to respond only to the rhythm as we do in the discotheque? Or will the movements reflect the melody? As high notes are heard, will the movements be done on a high level? Will the motion reflect the general mood of the composition?

The period from which the music comes and the style of the music will influence the movement. A pavane will, no doubt, elicit a stately response; an Irish jig will cause sprightly hops and jumps; a piece by Debussy may evoke a romantic mood. Electronic music is in some ways the easiest to use because it allows more freedom of interpretation.

Only after one has become comfortable with improvisation will one be able to turn on the music and dance.

RESPONDING TO COLORS

Although some will say that emotional response to colors is too abstract to serve beginners in movement improvisation, others will find it to be interesting. Just mention the word *red* or, if you like, stare at a piece of red construction paper. What comes to mind? Fire engines, fire, hot sun, Santa Claus, or what? React in movement.

RESPONDING TO OTHER SENSORY STIMULI

Response to texture can be intriguing if, without looking, one touches a substance such as ice, cotton, water, or sandpaper. Respond immediately in movement. Let other dancers guess the stimulus. Imagination of sensory stimuli will also serve. For example, imagine walking in deep snow, on soft sand, or on the moon.

Can you show gloom, happiness, fear, or pride in movement? Of course you can! We do it every day. But in the dance studio and later on the performance stage, these emotions must be made abstract and the essence of the feeling translated into movement. This is more difficult than one would think. Consider the general body position: is it expanded or contracted? Are the movements free or bound? Is the quality percussive, sustained, or swinging? Is the tempo fast or slow or in flux? Will the dimension of the space be constrained or expanded? These and other considerations will help in the translation of the expression of a mood to expressive dance. Martha Graham's *Lamentation* is one of the most moving examples of the use of body movement to express an emotion.

Figures 4–3 and 4–4 show the contrast between an internalized emotion such as grief and an expansive emotion such as pride.

FIGURE 4-3
Grief
Ken Roesser

FIGURE 4-4
Pride
Ken Roesser

REACTING TO A PARTNER

Move freely and explore spatial relationships. Try moving side by side, one following the other, meeting, passing, moving toward and away from each other, moving in unison or in opposition.

RELATING TO SPECIFIC BODY PARTS

Once again, utilize various parts of the body as motivation for movement. Each partner concentrates on only one part as he or she relates to one area of the partner's body. For example, elbow to heel or back to chin.

FIGURE 4-5
Back to chin
Ken Roesser

LITERAL VERSUS ABSTRACT MOVEMENTS

If you need to be literal, toss and catch an imaginary ball. Now toss and catch a feather or an elephant. Remember not to pantomine but to expand the natural gestures into larger, more abstract movements.

Now you are ready to toss a movement back and forth without a literal intent.

ANTIPHONAL MOVEMENTS

Partner A presents a movement phrase; partner B answers. The answer can be a new movement phrase or a replica or a variation of the original phrase. Continue or reverse the procedure.

MIRROR IMAGES

With a partner acting as your mirror image, explore the possibilities of moving as one. Without verbal communication you will find that one person will take the lead and the other will follow, at first. After a while, the other's movement will seem stronger, and the leadership shifts. Whatever the movement, the eyes of each partner must be focused on the other in order to maintain mirror-image movements.

GROUP IMPROVISATION

Group improvisation offers even greater challenges and rewards. Try some of the following suggestions:

FOLLOW THE LEADER

The leader must remain in front of the group, or at least the gaze must be forward even if the body turns, for the group attempts to follow the movements of the leader without hesitation and in unison. At first, choose a leader who is comfortable in improvisational movement. Members of the group will benefit in two ways. They will learn to move spontaneously, and they will also be forced to try movements which are natural to the leader and perhaps foreign to themselves. Change leaders, and the motion possibilities are different. If working with a large number of people, more than one group is more manageable. Then, the leaders can interact if desired.

SHIFTING GROUPS

Groups which are accustomed to improvisation and feel free to move in space will enjoy this exercise in group relationships. Begin in an arrangement of two trios and two quartets (this is an example for fourteen people). Dancers move within their assigned group, moving as independent individuals but relating to the others in the group. Members of each group are free to break away from their own groups at any time or to join another group. New numerical groupings are formed for a while, but these are always in flux. One's movements will reflect that of the group with which one is interacting.

Using an overhead projector to cast light on a wall in a darkened room, dancers moving in front of the wall will produce exciting shadows of shapes and forms. Everyone has done this with the fingers while waiting for a home slide show to begin.

With a group, one can produce many-headed and multilimbed creatures, ghostly scenes, and mock battles. One of the greatest advantages to this movement experience is that the darkened room eliminates inhibitions.

ADDITIONAL
SOURCES

Like all artists, there are times when one feels uninspired and unable to find sources of new movement. Look to past experiences for material. Many successful movement studies and dance compositions have been based on sports, folk dances, children's games, or work movements. These are all movement-based experiences that evoke emotional responses as well.

SPORTS

A baseball game is a great way to explore the contrast between axial and locomotor movement, use of directions in space (especially the diagonal), and dynamic contrasts of qualities of movement: swinging, percussive, and sustained.

FIGURE 4-6
A baseball game provides contrasts in movement
Marj Cox

Begin by pantomiming the actual sport movements. These movements can then be abstracted by altering some of the elements. For example, pitch the ball in slow motion; swing the bat with the whole body rather than just the arms; use the momentum of catching the ball to carry the body into a fall and roll on the floor.

If you involve the spectators as well, this becomes a marvelous example of the use of focus. And don't forget the emotional aspects of suspense, winning, and losing!

FOLK DANCE

George Balanchine's *Tarantella* shows how folk dance material can be developed into the classical ballet idiom in a beautiful composition. Modern dance students can begin with a well-known folk dance step such as the mazurka or the *Salty Dog Rag* and invent variations and additions.

WORK MOVEMENTS

Ted Shawn's *Labor Symphony* used work movements in an attempt to demonstrate to early twentieth-century America that men's dance could be virile and strong. Explore common work movements such as chopping, hammering, sweeping, shoveling, typing, and the like. You will discover that some are percussive, others are sustained. Axial movements can become locomotor and vice versa. Changes can be made in tempo, direction, dimension, and so on.

CHILDREN'S GAMES

Hopscotch, jump rope, "Ring Around the Roses," and statues all evoke movement memories in most of us. Take your partner by the hand, whirl him or her around a few times, and as he or she is flung away, watch for the unexpected shapes his or her posed body produces.

SCULPTURES

Another way to explore body shapes is to imagine your partner to be a lump of clay. Without verbal communication, mold this clay into a sculpture. Your gestures indicate where and how your partner is to move. You will learn about balance and line as well as emotional impact as your sculpture takes shape. Show it to others when you have a finished product. Now reciprocate by becoming a lump of clay. In this role, you will learn kinesthetically about balance and line as well, for if your sculptor poses you on one foot and then moves another part of your body out of line, you will experience fatigue in attempting to hold the distorted pose, or you will topple and have to be reshaped.

These suggestions are offered in the hope that they will stimulate your imagination and help you to think of other means of motivating improvisational movement. It will become easier in time and with practice. Evaluate what you have done or listen to the comments of others. But be aware that movement expression is personal, and your style may not be appreciated by everyone. Do not try to please, only strive for originality, clarity of communication, and continual growth in effective use of your instrument of expression.

5

CHOREOGRAPHY

You dance what you are,
or what you have become,
not merely what you wish to convey.[1]

Choreography, the composition of dances, is one of the
most rewarding personal experiences in modern dance.
The most successful choreography is produced when one
has a technically trained instrument, an understanding of
the elements of movement, the freedom to manipulate
these materials in unique ways, and an understanding of
how a dance is formed. This chapter introduces some of
the theories of the craft of choreography. But first, some
introductory remarks and background are needed.

You have understood and experienced the need for
technical training of the body in preparation for dance.
The materials of movement have been analyzed and explored in Chapters 3 and 4. In studying modern dance, you
have discovered its uniqueness in that the technical training of the instrument, and opportunities for the manipulation of materials of movement, occur simultaneously. The
neophyte in modern dance is encouraged to create movements and develop them into patterns and studies, and
eventually into dance form. In other types of dance,
opportunity to be both performer and creator comes after
years of study, and even then only to a few. Generally, in
ballet, for example, it is a creative experience for the
choreographer; for the dancer it is largely an interpretive
one. This is not always the case. Some choreographers give
their experienced dancers the opportunity to create parts

[1]Martha Graham, from a lecture to students at the Boston-Bouvé School of
Physical Education, Boston, in the 1940s.

FIGURE 5-1
Choreography:
a rewarding experience
Marj Cox

of their dances. Anthony Dowell has said that Frederick Ashton often encouraged him to improvise and then selected which movements to use.[2]

Beginning students should seize every opportunity to create dance movements, patterns, and dances, even before their bodies have achieved technical competence. Through experiencing the creative process, their minds will expand, and later, when their instruments are more finely tuned, so will be their creativity. These experiments in creative movements should not be substituted for technical training; the two facets of modern dance are of equal importance. Moreover, there must exist a reason for the dance. Life experience and study provide the dancer with something meaningful to communicate to an audience as well as the tools to do so. Once the reason for a dance has been established, some choreographers turn to music, narrative, or the spoken word for motivation. Other choreographers begin with a movement theme. In either event, improvisation is often the next step, followed by selection, rejection, alteration, and refinement, until movement patterns are finalized. The spontaneity of improvisation must be maintained during the selection and refinement process of choreography.

The line between improvisation and choreography is a difficult one to describe. Before considering the principles of composition, we must understand design, form,

[2]Anthony Dowell, from an interview on "Live From Lincoln Center," **PBS** television, May 28, 1980.

and style, three factors which are basic to any composition.

DESIGN In designing a dance, the choreographer coordinates past experiences and skills and the materials of movement with his or her present goal in an effort to produce a unified group of movements which can be called a composition. Among the considerations which contribute to the overall design of the piece are the spatial, temporal, and energy manipulations of motion and stillness.

FORM Form is that which has a definite shape or arrangement. We are told that art has form and that dance, as art, must have form. Form exists when the elements of movement (space, time, and force) are organized into a definite shape or arrangement so that the choreographer's intent is expressed. This is the major difference between improvised movement and a carefully structured composition. Louis Horst described form as "movement put into shape to perform."[3] The achievement of form in dance, or

FIGURE 5-2
Form is that which has
a definite shape
Marj Cox

[3]Louis Horst, from a lecture to a composition class at the Martha Graham School of Contemporary Dance, New York, 1948.

126

FIGURE 5-3
Paul Taylor
Jack Mitchell

in any artistic discipline, occurs in various ways. Students of composition are advised to experiment with different manners of working and to learn the rules established by experience and tradition; only later, after serving a term of obeyance to the rules, is it permissible to depart from them—just as when viewing Picasso's early representational art we realize that he first learned the rules before seemingly disregarding them.

A statement by Paul Taylor gives insight into one choreographer's use of form: "To me modern dance is a license to do what I feel is worth doing, without somebody saying that I can't do it because it does not fit into a category."[4]

STYLE   The style of a dance or of a dancer refers to the method of expression and results from uniqueness in manner of composition. Style is the conglomerate of many factors. In a dancer, anatomical limitations, technical training, emotional characteristics, and ethnic background all play a

[4]Paul Taylor, "Down With Choreography," in *The Modern Dance: Seven Statements of Belief,* ed. Selma Jeanne Cohen (Middletown, CT: Wesleyan University Press, 1966), p. 101.

FIGURES 5-4 and 5-5
Two duets: one abstract, the other comedy
Fig. 5-4 by David B. Moyer; Fig. 5-5 by Marj Cox

role. One speaks of a dancer as having a ballet style, a jazz style, a Spanish style, or a Graham or a Limon style of moving.

Contemporary dancers strive to rid themselves of stylistic affectations to which they have been exposed and to develop unique styles of moving which are suitable to the intent of the specific dance being performed.

The style of a dance is a reflection of the intent of the choreographer. The design and form, the method of manipulating the components of movement, the choice of accompaniment, the choice of dancers, and the stylization of their movements must all enhance the underlying idea which is to be communicated. If it is to be a period piece or an ethnic dance, the style of movement will reflect that which was evident in a given historical time or place. The most successful choreographers have been those capable of presenting an evening of dance in which each piece reflects its own style.

PRINCIPLES OF COMPOSITION

The Reason for the Dance: The Idea Theme

In order to communicate to others, you must first clearly understand what you want to say. If it can be said in words, in pantomime, or through another medium, perhaps it is not an adequate reason for a dance composition. A dance, to be meaningful, must express the core of the dancer's intent, the way the dancer feels about his or her theme. The reason for a dance can be an idea, a thought, a mood, a story, or just the development of movement for its own sake. Contemporary modern dance is often concerned with pure movement, and there are no preconceived expectations for audience response except that each person derive whatever meaning he or she finds in viewing the piece.

The beginning choreographer has a higher chance for success if he or she chooses a rather simple theme and treats a clearly defined concept with depth, rather than attempting an all-encompassing or extreme theme such as "the history of civilization." The choreographer must also be familiar with his or her theme in order to do it justice.

In addition, a choreographer must consider the technical competence of the dancer or dancers who will perform the piece. Beginning dancers will be more successful communicating a straightforward theme rather than one which is too subtle. Doris Humphrey reminds us that "big ideas and meager equipment are not very good mates."[5]

The reasons for dance change with the times, like clothing fashions. A creative artist chooses whether to abide by today's fashions in choreography or to be a trailblazer. If one chooses the latter, one risks nonacceptance. If the former is chosen, one must avoid being a "copy cat." *Swan Lake* and the *Nutcracker* have been more than adequately choreographed, as have *Rodeo* and *Cry*. Beginning choreographers may choose a theme which is similar to one they have seen performed, but they do not possess the skill to treat a theme which has been created by a master with enough originality to be unique.

[5]Doris Humphrey, *The Art of Making Dances*, ed. Barbara Pollack (New York: Rinehart & Co., 1959), p. 95.

The Movement Theme

Once the idea theme has been chosen, the choreographer develops a movement theme or motif. This often becomes the first phrase of movement in the dance, or sometimes it evolves gradually. In either case, the movement theme contains the generic information from which the dance develops. It is wise to be highly critical of the movement theme, since it provides the germ from which the rest of the movement grows. Is it interesting? Does it mean what is intended? Does it offer development possibilities? At this point, the ideational theme may be rejected as undanceable. If so, choose another and begin again. In developing the movement theme, avoid utilizing all available material at once or there will be nothing left for development.

The Development: The Beginning, the Middle, and the Ending

It is generally accepted that most compositions, whether music, writing, or dance, should have a beginning, a middle, and an ending. We have discussed the beginning: the statement of a movement theme. The middle comprises the development of the implied material. In developing a movement motif, one manipulates the various components of movement through the use of the elements of space, time, and force. Avoid using movements, steps, or techniques which have been learned in class; these are merely exercises useful in training the body. If they are used as choreographic materials, the result will be a routine, not a creative composition. This is not to imply that the basic locomotor and axial movements which are part of technique class are taboo. Paul Taylor's *Esplanade* is an example of the integration of locomotor movements in an exciting composition. Also, avoid using movements you have seen others do. Be inventive. Find movements which are unique to you and which are tailor-made for the thematic development of your dance.

The climax of a dance occurs when one section is emphasized. This can be done in innumerable ways: by increasing the dynamics, the tempo, the duration, or the use of space, for example. The climax of the composition may occur in the middle section or may be closer to the end. Often, following the climax there is a resolution, but this is not always the case. There may be more than one climax, if desired.

The ending may include a return to the beginning material, or it may present a summation or a resolution. Sometimes the ending is purposely left unresolved. The ending of the dance is perhaps the most important part, for it is the part most likely to be remembered by the audience. Yet in many compositions it is the weakest. Avoid just falling to the floor or spinning off stage if there is no previous justification for these movements in the theme. The ending should not appear to be "tacked on" at the end like the donkey's tail; it should be a meaningful part of the choreography.

The three parts need not necessarily be created in the above order. Some choreographers find that the beginning and ending come easily and what to do in between is the problem; or, a dancer might have the whole dance in mind except an idea of how to begin! The development is aided by the choreographer's ideas, by the actual material within the movement theme, and by other helpful devices such as accompaniment, costume ideas, number of dancers who will perform, and the available space. Movement, however, is the material of dance and must be the major concern at all times. Be ever mindful of the movement theme, and try to be faithful to its implications as the theme is developed. Too much material will cause confusion.

AESTHETIC PRINCIPLES

The aesthetic principles of composition are applicable to dance as they are to other art forms. The following is a brief explanation of some of these. For a more complete review consult Hayes and H'Doubler.[6]

Unity

For a dance composition to have unity, the choreographer chooses his movement material carefully and weeds out superfluous material which does not contribute to the general movement theme. Unity is also achieved by the treatment of the chosen material and by attention to the following principles.

[6]For a more complete review of aesthetic principles, see Elizabeth R. Hayes, *Dance Composition and Production for High Schools and Colleges* (New York: The Ronald Press Company, 1955), pp. 11–21; and Margaret N. H'Doubler, *Dance: A Creative Art Experience* (New York: Appleton-Century-Crofts, 1940), pp. 135–148.

CONTRAST AND VARIATION

In an effort to adhere to the principle of unity, one must not allow one's movements, use of space, rhythms, or dynamics to become monotonous. The proper amount of contrast and variation of specific elements will help to avoid this pitfall. There is no end to the possible ways in which these elements can be manipulated, but one must choose variations carefully so that the original material is still clear. Contrast and variation are also achieved by the arrangement of dancers, or groups of dancers.

REPETITION

Frequently it is helpful to repeat sections of a dance for emphasis. It is comforting for an audience to recognize a recurring theme, and it helps the choreographer to state his intent. As long as the repetitiveness is not overdone, it is a useful device.

SEQUENCE

The sequence of movement must follow a logical pattern, but not one that is so predictable as to become mundane. For example, four hops on the left foot do not necessarily need to be followed by four hops on the right foot. The sequence can be more subtle. The use of sequential movement helps the audience to follow the general pattern leading to a climax and conclusion.

TRANSITION

Transitional passages serve as bridges between movement, phrases of movement, or sections of a dance. Transitions help in the development of the motif stated in the first section and in relating one section to another. Sometimes a transition consists of a movement which seems to flow from the preceding to the following movement. It can relate more closely to one or the other. Occasionally a transition occurs as stillness, perhaps the holding of a shape. Transitions can be long or short. The audience may or may not be aware of them, but when the transitions are missing, the dance often becomes simply a group of movements strung together.

BALANCE

In dance, balance has different meanings. In composition, balance is achieved through the ways in which the elements of movement are manipulated, by the arrangement of one's body parts, and also by the arrangement of dancers in a group or groups. When the movements or relationships of dancers are symmetrical, balance is achieved; if asymmetrical, a lack of balance is the result. Balance of movement phrases and sections is also to be considered in the longer pieces.

The ways in which a dancer achieves and maintains balance in stillness and in motion are discussed in Chapter 3. From the time of one's first dance technique class, it is only by achieving balance of body parts that one manages to overcome the force of gravity.

SIMPLICITY

Let us not forget that often the most simply stated materials are the most meaningful. One frequently becomes so involved with subject matter, rules for proceeding, and the abundance of materials that one tries to include everything in one composition. The beauty of a single rose is sometimes more breathtaking than that of a bouquet of roses. A simple, well-defined statement in movement will often carry a greater impact than a piece which includes more than an audience can grasp in a fleeting moment.

It is the harmony that results from thoughtful attention to the above factors that helps a choreographer to achieve a meaningful composition which is an artistic expression of his or her intent. Whether the aim is to communicate a story, an emotion, or an idea, or whether it is to communicate the kinetic experience which results from the manipulation of movement for its own sake, consideration of these principles will be helpful to the beginning choreographer. More experienced choreographers often appear to disregard the "rules" but achieve the same ends. It is important to remember that communication in dance depends on having something to say, the ability to be expressive, technical competence in movement, and the skillful and harmonious manipulation of movement materials.

MUSICAL FORMS

Dancers frequently depend upon musical forms as aids in composition. Louis Horst taught Martha Graham and hundreds of her followers the relationship of musical forms to dance composition. His choice of preclassic dance forms was made because of their simple, uncluttered formality. His course in preclassic dance forms began in 1928 at the Neighborhood Playhouse in New York. He later developed a course in modern forms. Horst's books are highly recommended.[7]

The following is a summary of some musical forms which are helpful to choreographers.

Sequential Form

Sequential form consists of more than one part. It is suitable for either solo or group compositions. Each part is a unit, with its own theme, and one follows the other. A short dance may consist of only one section which is a complete statement. This is often called period form.

BINARY (AB)

A. The first section consists of a statement and development of movement material.

B. The second section is again a statement, usually in some way a contrast to A. In spite of the difference in the material, it is generally related to or implied by the material found in A and often completes the material in the A section.

TERNARY (ABA or ABC)

In ABA form, A and B are complete and separate thematic statements. When A recurs, it may be a repetition of the original A, or it may be somewhat altered by the proximity of the B material. A comparison can be made: when a person lives in a foreign land for a few years and then returns to his or her native land, there are some residual changes in that person because of the foreign experience.

In ABC form, there are three separate thematic statements.

[7]Louis Horst, *Pre-Classic Dance Forms* (New York: Dance Horizons, 1968, reprint), and Louis Horst and Carrol Russell, *Modern Dance Forms* (San Francisco: Impulse Publications, 1961).

A. The theme consists of a short, meaningful, but simple statement.

A$_1$, A$_2$, and so on. The sections which follow are variations of that theme. Usually the first is the most similar to the theme. Perhaps the movement is done on another level, in a new direction, or with a change in tempo, mood, or dynamics.

RONDO (ABACADA)

A. The original section states the main material. It is similar to the chorus of a song and is repeated after each section of new material, which constitutes the verses (B, C, D, etc.). The chorus or A section can be altered slightly but should not deviate too far from its original statement. The dance usually ends with a restatement of the original material.

Contrapuntal Forms

These forms are useful in group compositions. More than one movement theme is used simultaneously. Each theme should be a simple one so that it remains recognizable whether presented alone, in combination, or in juxtaposition with others.

CANON

The canon form requires at least two dancers. The first dancer presents a movement theme. After a designated time (perhaps a phrase of movement), a second dancer begins with the original theme and follows through with the same material as the first dancer, but always a phrase behind. Other dancers may follow in like manner. In the canon form, sometimes the original theme is slightly altered during subsequent introductions. Occasionally, the canon ends with a coda in which all dancers do unison movement.

ROUND

The round is a form of canon in which the successive entrances of dancers are often somewhat further apart; therefore, the movement phrase is longer. It is a popular form for children's songs such as "Three Blind Mice." The first dancer presents a movement phrase. As he or she begins the second movement phrase, a second dancer begins the first phrase of movement. As the first dancer begins a third phrase and the second dancer begins the second phrase, a third dancer enters with the first phrase. When the first and second dancers complete the three parts of the dance, each waits until the third dancer is also finished. The same system applies when groups rather than single dancers are involved.

FUGUE

A number of themes are introduced by different dancers or groups of dancers. The original theme prevails throughout the composition in spite of the addition of other themes, variations, and developments. At some point there is generally a climax, followed by a recapitulation of the original theme.

Freedom from Form

Contemporary dancers often seem to disregard all rules of composition. There appears to be no adherence to one of the preceding musical forms. Instead, the form results from the underlying intent of the choreographer. It is more difficult to compose without guidelines, and therefore most beginners are well advised to work within a frame-work. The reader is referred to Margery Turner,[8] who discusses alternate methods of establishing form in dance composition.

CHOREOGRAPHY BY CHANCE (ALEATORY)

Merce Cunningham introduced the concept of aleatory, or choreography by chance, on the concert stage. It is a device well suited for the studio as well. Here is one way to try it. Put several pieces of paper in a box. On each is a movement suggestion, such as: move in a circular pattern, perform a percussive movement, move on a low level, execute a movement with an uneven $\frac{3}{4}$ meter, etc. Each student or group of students draws three or four slips of paper from the box and then retires to a corner of the

[8]Margery J. Turner, *New Dance: Approaches to Nonliteral Choreography* (Pittsburgh: University of Pittsburgh Press, 1971).

FIGURE 5-6
Merce Cunningham
in *Changeling* (1957)
Richard Rutledge

studio to compose a movement study based on the suggestions. For beginning choreographers the ideas furnish a base on which to build movement, a set of directions as to how to proceed. Later, transitions can be developed and refinements made.

GROUP CHOREOGRAPHY

There are two types of group choreography. The first is choreography done by a group for the group. The other is choreography done by one individual for a group of dancers. The first type is more common in an educational setting, in which a group of students is charged with the task of creating a movement study or even a complete dance. In professional companies, this is less likely to be the case. A notable exception is the Pilobolus Dance Theatre, which began in 1971 when three Dartmouth students, nondancers, became interested in a unique and interesting form of creative movement.

When a group of individuals engage in the process of creating a unified piece, several factors must be considered. It is important that the size of the group not be too large, lest the process be lengthy and difficult. If a large group is divided into smaller groups and each is assigned to work on a segment of the dance, that problem is sometimes resolved; however, stylistic differences often result. When members of the group are not at the same level of technical skill or choreographic competence, the more skilled dancers tend to assume leadership. Other times, those with more aggressive personalities emerge as leaders. If the result desired is a group effort, members must listen to and consider the suggestions of each individual. Compromises must be made. Constructive criticism must be given and accepted. Each contributor must remain mindful of the chosen theme of the dance and be willing to disregard personal preferences when they seem unsuited to the total project. Much is learned about dance, as well as about interpersonal relations, when a project such as this is successfully accomplished. After the various suggestions are put together, adaptations must be made to ensure unity of style and adherence to the original theme of the piece.

In professional companies, the more common arrangement is that one choreographer arranges a piece for a group of dancers which may or may not include the choreographer. Students should also be given opportunities to experience this manner of choreography. When one individual choreographs for a group of dancers, there are different considerations. The movement style tends to be that of the choreographer and therefore will likely be consistent throughout. The technical competence of the dancers who will perform the work must be considered, as well as their personal styles. Will they be able to adapt to the style and technical demands of the choreographer? Paul Taylor has observed, "The finest choreography in the world does not mean a thing if the dancers are not suited to it and they look terrible."[9]

The choreographer must be able to visualize group relationships of dancers in the space to be utilized. He or she must be adaptable to suggestions from the dancers when ideas are translated into actualities or when they fail to occur as planned. The number of dancers to be included will affect the overall design of the piece. Balance, floor patterns, groupings, and sequential movements are only a few considerations. The larger the number of dancers used, the simpler the movement should be. The statement

[9]Paul Taylor, "Down With Choreography," in *The Modern Dance: Seven Statements of Belief*, ed. Selma Jeanne Cohen (Middletown, CT: Wesleyan University Press, 1966), p. 91.

will be projected by numbers, and too much busy work will produce confusion rather than clarity.

Working with a group of dancers offers many more possibilities than working with only one or two. The design of axial movements and floor patterns and the use of contrast, harmony, unity, and succession are only a few of the many factors to be considered. Large groups of dancers can move in unison or can be divided into smaller groups, including solos, duets, trios, quartets, and the like, Unison movement makes a strong statement, but it must not be continued too long. Groups moving in contrasting movements present greater possibilities for interesting patterns. Having individual dancers repeat movements sequentially, like the fall of dominoes, is an effective device but should be used sparingly lest it become monotonous.

Symmetrical and asymmetrical arrangements of persons within groups will suggest uniformity or contrast. The shape of a group is also indicative of the intended motivation. A circle is most serene, often suggestive of a ritual; a "clump" may appear haphazard; a file is regimental; and a line of dancers in a row moving in unison suggests a chorus line. When dancers move out of such rigid arrangements, more unusual spatial patterns result. The amount of space between dancers, the placement of groups on stage, the direction in which each dancer moves, and the number of dancers in each subgroup are only a few of the constantly shifting considerations that help create the design of the dance.

When several groups on stage are simultaneously engaged in different movement patterns employing vari-

FIGURE 5-7
A group of dancers
offers many
interesting possibilities
David B. Moyer

ous spatial designs, contrasts of dynamics, and perhaps even different rhythmic patterns, one must be cautious that everything has a unified intent. Beware of the three-ring-circus effect that causes the confused viewers to wonder which group to watch. Sometimes the intention of the choreographer is to focus attention on a soloist, using other dancers as a chorus, or to highlight one group and then another.

Before completing a dance composition, it is wise to consider Doris Humphrey's advice to choreographers which is as pertinent to today's dance as ever.

Symmetry is lifeless
Two-dimensional design is lifeless
The eye is faster than the ear
Movement looks slower and weaker on the stage
All dances are too long
A good ending is forty percent of the dance
Monotony is fatal; look for contrasts
Don't be a slave to, or a mutilator of, the music
Listen to qualified advice; don't be arrogant
Don't intellectualize; motivate movement
Don't leave the ending to the end[10]

[10]Doris Humphrey, *The Art of Making Dances*, p. 159. Each of these statements is elaborated in this book.

6
PERFORMANCE

There are many reasons for dance, among them communication, artistic expression, entertainment, recreation, physical fitness, and therapy. Adults who elect to study modern dance may be doing so for any of these reasons. If recreation or therapy is your goal, you may have little need to perform. Taking class, exploring movement, and learning to perform movement patterns will suffice. However, if your goal is to communicate to others through movement, dance must be performed. No matter how limited in technical competence, students can find satisfaction in the choreography and presentation of their own dances. Informal presentations within the class or demonstrations and workshops can answer this need.

For more gifted or more highly trained technicians, the opportunity to participate in a concert situation is important. A performance serves as a climax after months of preparation. During this time, the dancer brings his or her instrument to peak form, the choreographer shapes and reshapes the flow of movements which eventually become a dance, and then the dancers learn and polish the finished dance. Much thought, time, and effort is expended by dancers and ancillary people in order to produce a dance concert. The result is worth the effort, for the satisfactions are numerous.

Even in an educational setting, performance opportunities are justified, providing that the preparations do not detract from the educational benefits. Class time must not be devoted to rehearsals. Some students seek the opportunity to choreograph or to perform. Others are inclined to benefit from the rewards of dance in the studio only; thus, performing must not be thrust upon everyone.

FIGURE 6-1
A performance
serves as a climax
David B. Moyer

Some students will find satisfaction in "behind the scenes" contributions.

In high schools and colleges, dance classes are usually geared to learning the techniques and components of dance, while performance opportunities are available in extracurricular dance groups. In this way, the more advanced students are provided the opportunities they seek. In some schools, auditions are required for dance group membership; in other schools, all who wish to join are accepted.

Depending on the format of the performance, whether it be an informal workshop or demonstration or a more formal concert, and on the size of the audience and whether or not an admission charge is required, the demands on the dancers vary greatly. In general, the smaller and the more intimate the presentation, the less demanding it is.

Although movement is the primary ingredient in the preparation of a dance for performance, other factors support and enhance the choreography and are therefore worthy of study. The following discussion is presented to stimulate your thinking so that you may creatively manipulate the supportive effects of sound, lighting, and other visual effects to augment your choreography. Additional help can be obtained from reading *Dance Production*,[1]

[1]Gertrude Lippincott, "Planning and Rehearsing a Dance Program," in *Dance Production*, ed. Gertrude Lippincott (Washington: American Association for Health, Physical Education and Recreation, 1956, 1960).

especially Chapter 2, and *A Guide to Dance Production: "On With the Show."*[2]

ACCOMPANIMENT

Dance and music have been partners for centuries. Today's modern dance does not depend as heavily on music as dance did in earlier times. Still, most dancers utilize music or sound as accompaniment. The choice of accompaniment should be a careful one so as not to allow the dance to be subservient to music. Instead, the dance and its accompaniment should work together, each enhancing the other.

Not all choreographers have the good fortune to be able to commission scores for their dances. Instead, most are required to find ready-made accompaniment and then create the dance, or to create the dance and then search for suitable music. One tends to choose music which is composed, orchestrated, or arranged for one or more instruments, recorded, and readily available. To avoid difficulties with this decision, consider the following:

> Some music is self-sufficient. The composer has stated his intent so completely that it would be difficult to create dance movement which would add to the statement. Music for a full orchestra often has so much going on that only a "cast of thousands" type of dance group could do justice to this accompaniment.

> Recorded music with vocalists may cause the audience to listen to the words and expect the dancer to interpret literally the same intent. If this is not your purpose, choose music without lyrics. The music chosen must be immediately enjoyable by the audience, who will hear it only once. The choreographer and dancers, however, will hear it hundreds of times, so it must be tolerable for many repetitions.

If recorded or orchestral music is not suitable to your dance idea, investigate alternate means of accompaniment. Electronic scores or music played by percussion instruments can be more abstract and therefore less restrictive. Percussive accompaniment is readily available in

[2]*A Guide to Dance Production: On With the Show.* Reston, VA: National Dance Association of the American Alliance for Health, Physical Education, Recreation and Dance, 1981.

the form of a drum, cymbals, triangles, and the like. Even a metronome furnishes an interesting, though stark, accompaniment. One's own ingenuity will occasionally enable one to devise percussive sounds using miscellaneous equipment such as metal wastebaskets, rice in a tin box, or anything that happens to be around! Body sounds and voice sounds have been used as dance accompaniment since before the development of musical instruments and are still suitable. The spoken word, with or without background music, is another good possibility. Beware of dancing while speaking because of breathing difficulties; a nondancing speaker, a chorus of speakers, or a recorded voice is more practical.

Some dancers have choreographed dances with no sound, only the occasional rhythmic sounds of the feet on the stage, or other body sounds, such as claps or snaps of the fingers. José Limon's *The Unsung* and The Pilobolus's *Walklyndon* are striking examples of unaccompanied movement. This is often an effective means to intensify movement appreciation. Some audiences, however, accustomed to the marriage of sound and movement, find this difficult to comprehend.

Some choreographers prefer to create the dance and then search for suitable accompaniment. This method allows more freedom during the choreographic process. The accompaniment chosen will then be one which will enhance the statement of the dance. Some choreographers are concerned with matching musical form, rhythmic structure, and duration of the music with the dance. Others choose accompaniment which is less closely related but which subtly adds to the general effect. Whatever the process, that which is chosen for the dance should not just accompany the dance but should become an integral part of the total composition.

In performance, presentation of music is often an economic rather than an artistic decision. Of course it would be lovely to dance in a theatre with an orchestra or ensemble of skilled musicians in the pit or with a virtuoso pianist at the Steinway Grand on stage, but more often dancers must be content with prerecorded music. One must be certain that the sound quality is agreeable to the ears of the audience, or it will detract from the visual effect of the dance.

If using a record, remember to buy two—one for the innumerable times it will be played during choreography and rehearsal and the other for taping before the performance.

All music should be taped on a previously unused tape. Pieces should be arranged in the order of appearance, and if more than one tape is required, reel changes should be done during intermissions.

Think how disconcerting it would be to a dancer, on stage, in opening pose, to hear the music start two bars after the beginning! This can easily happen when records are used; those two bars and all your meaningful movement have vanished forever.

When the spoken voice is the accompaniment for a dance, a more reliable performance is achieved if the speaker makes a tape. The timing will be certain, and the possibility of a laryngitis on opening night is avoided.

Backup equipment and duplicate tapes are a must. This is even more necessary when performing away from home base. And don't forget to take along a wall plug adapter and an extension cord!

Before the performance begins, the technician should check sound levels for both the audience and the dancers. It is also wise to tape any loose cords to the floor to prevent accidents when dancers rush on and off stage.

CHOOSING A TITLE

A title or program notes help to prepare an audience for what to expect. The title of the ballet *The Sleeping Beauty* implies just that. Modern dance titles have not always been so helpful. If it is your intent to let the dance speak for itself and to mean different things to different people, then you are wise to choose a title such as "Opus 15" or "Untitled Work." However, if your intention is that the dance be considered to be symbolic of a preconceived idea, then give the audience a clue: "Satyrs" or "Three Moods." Sometimes the title of the music is used as the title of the dance as well. George Balanchine frequently does this with success, for he utilizes the structure of the music. But for students it is best not to follow suit, for it usually implies inability to think of a title. Be sure the title you choose is thoughtfully considered. Walter Sorell suggests that a title is like a first impression when we meet a new person.[3]

While the title should suggest what is to follow, it must not say everything or the dance will be superfluous. It is better if the title can suggest but leave the audience the feeling of anticipation. Titles are important! Don't just throw something together such as "Blue Moods" because on the day of the printer's deadline for program information it happens to be a gloomy Monday morning and you can't think of anything else!

Program notes are sometimes useful when the choreographer feels that words will enhance the audience's understanding of his or her intent. Brevity is advised. In most cases, a dance should speak for itself kinesthetically.

COSTUMES Partly because of parsimony and also because of an artistic desire for simplicity, modern dancers tend to costume their dances sparsely. From Isadora Duncan's simple robe to Martha Graham's "long woolen's" period to today's unencumbered unitard or nude look, an effort has been made to prevent the costume from interfering with or distracting from movement of the body.

The design of the costume is important in continuing the line of the body and can either contribute to or detract from the choreographic intent.

For dramatic purposes there are ways to alter a basic leotard which even the most stringent budget will allow. The addition of skirts, sleeves, collars, stripes, ribbons, sashes, vests, and so on, can add color and also be suggestive of the mood of the dance. Ingenuity is more important than funds in effective costuming. Special effects can be sewn, glued, or painted onto the leotard. One word of caution: Be sure that all additions are carefully secured lest they fall off during a performance. Even a small item such as a sequin can cause a dancer to slip on the stage. When special effects such as confetti, straw, or artificial snow are needed, make sure that the stage is meticulously swept before the next number in the performance.

[3]Walter Sorell, *The Dancer's Image: Points and Counterpoints* (New York and London: Columbia University Press, 1971), p. 33.

In selecting the material for costumes, it must be remembered that the body will be in motion and therefore seams can split, buttons can pop, and headpieces are likely to fall off. Texture is also important in contributing to the desired mood. Costumes must be seen under stage lights in order to avoid surprises on opening night.

Frequently, costumes are designed and produced by the dancers or the choreographer. Other students, parents, or alumni can be enlisted to help. The deadline for completion must be the time of the technical rehearsal so that the lighting can be evaluated in terms of its effect on the costumes. By the time of the dress rehearsal, every detail of the costume must be in place, not only to assure that all parts of the costume are ready but also so that complete costume changes between numbers can be timed. There are occasions when a dancer may be required to wear one pair of tights under another, just to cut out five seconds of costume-changing time!

It is not always practical to wear the full costume during many rehearsals of a dance, but a reasonable facsimile should be used if the costume will alter the way a dancer moves. For example, if a long skirt is to be used, the dancer should practice for many weeks wearing a long skirt of similar material.

Hair styles should also be considered. In romantic ballet we are accustomed to Taglioni's neatly parted and pulled-back coiffure with buns on both sides or one in back. Martha Graham and other modern dancers sometimes use the flow of long hair to enhance the movement line of the body. Whatever the hair style indicated by the dance, one should be certain that it remain in place. Dancers who brush hair out of their eyes are using gestures which are not part of the choreography and have no justification.

At performance time, don't forget to have a sewing kit, safety pins, and bobby pins backstage.

The reader is referred to *A Guide to Dance Production: "On With the Show,"* Chapters 3 and 4 for more detail on the design and execution of costumes.[4]

---

[4]*A Guide to Dance Production: On With the Show,* Chapters 3 and 4 by Elizabeth R. Hayes. Reston, VA: National Dance Association of the American Alliance for Health, Physical Education, Recreation and Dance, 1981.

MAKEUP For centuries women have understood the psychological benefits of makeup. In the theatre, makeup has been used to help establish the characters being portrayed. In dance, which tends to be more abstract, the need for and use of makeup varies according to the intent of the dance and the setting in which the dance is being presented. If performing in a gymnasium or studio without stage lighting, or outdoors in daylight, only street makeup for the women and a touch of the same for the men is needed. When performing on a stage with special lighting, heavier makeup is essential to ensure that the features of dancers will be apparent. Depending on the color of the lights being used for the dance, makeup needs will vary. The coloring of the dancer's skin and how it is affected by the stage lighting are also considerations, and for that reason makeup should be tried on at the dress rehearsal, just as the costumes are. Why wait until the performance to find out that Susie appears to have no eyes at all?

Most women have had some experience with makeup, own some of their own, and often prefer to apply it themselves. A makeup "expert" should check everyone anyway, so that some uniformity results. Men usually welcome some help.

For character roles in dance, such as clowns, animals, or abstract nonhuman figures, makeup must be thoughtfully designed and carefully applied.

The placement on the program of dances which require heavy or special makeup must be considered, as the time needed to apply and remove it may be lengthy.

Too much makeup can be as disconcerting to the audience as too little. The effect must be determined before the performance by viewers stationed in the front row as well as in the back row of the auditorium or performing space.

There is an excellent chapter on makeup in *Dance Production* which includes a list of essential items to be included in a makeup box.[5]

---

[5]Eleanor Lauer, "An Introduction to Makeup for Dance Students," in *Dance Production*, ed. Gertrude Lippincott (Washington, D.C.: American Association for Health, Physical Education, and Recreation, 1956, 1960), pp. 57-64.

Dance can be and has been performed everywhere! Theatre dance began in the ballroom, with the spectators on both sides and the royalty often seated on a dais at the end of the room. The choreography emphasized spatial patterns. In the seventeenth century, when ballet was moved to the proscenium stage with the audience seated in front on a lower level, movements of the feet and legs were emphasized. For years, most theatrical dance has taken place in such theatres. Since the 1960s contemporary dancers have often preferred less formal spaces, such as lofts, gymnasiums, grassy hills, football fields, or museums. Dance can be performed wherever space permits. Audiences can be arranged in different ways, and sometimes audiences are even asked to change location during a performance. If the performance is to be done "in the round," choreography should be planned with that in mind, if possible. Touring groups find it necessary to adapt to many varieties of performing spaces.

Needless to say, most dancers require more space than they are usually allowed. If possible, the dance should be choreographed with some thought to the limitations of the performing space, but this is not always possible if the dance is to remain in the repertory and be

FIGURE 6-2
Performing
in a shopping plaza
Marj Cox

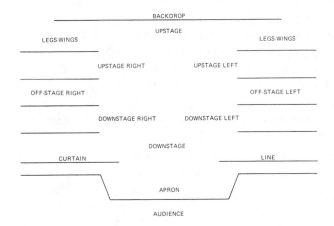

BACKDROP

UPSTAGE

LEGS-WINGS   LEGS-WINGS

UPSTAGE RIGHT   UPSTAGE LEFT

OFF-STAGE RIGHT   OFF-STAGE LEFT

DOWNSTAGE RIGHT   DOWNSTAGE LEFT

DOWNSTAGE

CURTAIN   LINE

APRON

AUDIENCE

FIGURE 6-3
Proscenium stage
Henry Duffy

FIGURE 6-4
A platform adds to the three
dimensionality of movement.
Marj Cox

performed on tour. Occasionally a situation may occur in
which the space is too large to do justice to the subtleties
of the movement or the spatial patterns. A more likely
situation is one in which the number of dancers required
by the dance simply will not fit in the space given.

Dramatic implications of the stage must also be
considered. It is generally agreed that the strongest area of
the stage is the center and the sides the weakest.

Risers, boxes, stairs, or platforms which add to the
three-dimensionality of movement are often used to great
advantage, especially in group dances. Such equipment is
often available in the theatre or can be custom-made by
the school carpenter or by students.

The surface of the floor is a primary consideration,
especially since many modern dancers prefer the freedom
of bare feet. There is no substitute for a good wooden floor;
tile and cement floors can be damaging to the feet and
legs, carpeting is often there to mask something undesira-
ble underneath, and outdoor surfaces are, at best, incon-
sistent. Even a good wooden floor such as one finds in an
auditorium or theatre must be properly prepared for

dancers. Cleanliness is essential. Last-minute sweeping must be done to remove dust, splinters, tacks, pins, bobby pins, crumbs, and all the extraneous accumulations of even a prepared floor. Custodians must be notified in advance not to wax the floor, lest it be too slippery; they sometimes seem to think of it at the wrong moment, even if the floor hasn't been waxed for years! Some groups travel with their own portable floor covering.

It seems too obvious to mention that uninvolved scenery, chairs, lecterns, and the like must be removed from the stage and wings. Entrance and exit passageways must be completely free of storage, for these areas are often used hastily and in darkness.

When touring, it is essential that allowance be made for rehearsal time in the performance space. Dancers must adjust to the spatial and textural differences of the area. They must also reorient themselves to the arrangement of exits and entrances and the time expended en route to and from dressing rooms.

SCENERY, PROPS, AND LIGHTING

Scenery generally must be kept to a minimum because of lack of space on stage. A simple curtain as a backdrop, with interesting lighting effects, will not only suffice but likely enhance most modern dance productions. Unlike romantic ballets like *Giselle*, in which scenery is essential to inform the audience of the time and place of the action, the modern dance audience need only be given a clean, uncluttered space which will not detract from movements dynamically designed in time and space. Although one may envy Martha Graham, who has the unsurpassed talent of Isamu Noguchi to design symbolic sculptures and sets, students can often find other talented students who are eager to show their creations and therefore willing to contribute sets or props.

Props can be used to further the intent of the dance or to increase the spatial possibilities of the dancer. Alwin Nikolais is most innovative in designing props and costumes which enhance the motion of the dancers. In the studio, explore movement in relation to hoops, balls, ribbons, ropes, chairs, balance beams, volley ball standards, or whatever is available. While props can serve as encumbrances in some ways, they also can expand the

FIGURE 6-5
A simple curtain
with interesting lighting
is sufficient.
Claire Dudly

FIGURE 6-6
A prop can increase
movement and spatial
possibilities.
Marj Cox

FIGURE 6-7
"Tensile Involvement"
from *Divertissment*
by Alwin Nikolais.
*Chinera photo. Used by
permission of Nikolais-Louis
Foundation for Dance*

imaginative use of the body in space. Andy Warhol's helium-filled pillows in Merce Cunningham's *Rain Forest* move about interacting with the dancers.

Proper lighting can also produce effects that enhance the central idea of the dance. If the stage is small, lighting has an advantage over scenery and props in that it does not intrude on dancing space.

In the design of lighting for dance, there are special considerations. Color and intensity play major roles in creating the desired mood for the dance. The placement of the beams of light can alter the illusion of the size or shape of the stage. The lighting should not remain static throughout an entire dance. Dimming, brightening, color changes, and other effects will accent the choreography. To coordinate quick changes, the lighting technician must know the dance nearly as well as the dancers do. When the choreography calls for a soloist to emerge from the group and to be highlighted, this must take place exactly on count one of the soloist's section, not three counts after he or she has begun. Lighting effects are, of course, limited by the equipment available in the auditorium. When a stage with good lighting facilities is available, many interesting effects can be achieved. Moods can be created. Colors of costumes can be altered or enhanced. Sunrise, sunset, darkness, and other effects can be approximated. In addition to using fixed spotlights and footlights, special effects can be achieved with moving spotlights, colored gels, slide projectors, overhead projectors, and various other devices such as the strobe or black light.

It is prudent if the choreographer does not depend too heavily on lighting to enhance his or her creation, since many dance concerts are held in gymnasiums or studios, out-of-doors, or in other "unlightable" spaces. In the harsh glare of the noonday sun, the dancer must rely upon his or her movement alone.

At the beginning of the twentieth century, Loie Fuller's reputation was established by her manipulation of voluminous costumes and the effect of lights on the materials. Alwin Nikolais achieves unusual and dramatic effects by uniting movement, costuming, lighting, slides, and sound in a multimedia art form. Other contemporary dancers have united the visual arts and dance in unique ways.

In becoming a modern dance artist, the choice is yours, whether to make a statement using only the movement of the unencumbered human body or to draw upon supportive media.

THE PROGRAM

Whenever two or more dances are to be presented, the order of appearance must be carefully considered. Many factors influence this decision, but the effect on the audience should be a major concern. It is usually advisable to open the performance with a light, sprightly piece, one which is not too long and the one most likely to please the most people! Thought-provoking dances and those requiring the audience's concentration belong in the middle. Save the "best" piece for last, for the impression made by the closing number will accompany the audience out into the night and all the way home.

Practical considerations such as which dancers appear in which dances and how fast they can change costumes and catch their breath are not to be minimized. Injuries and fainting spells are not worth the delight of seeing Susie in three successive pieces.

Once the order has been established, rehearse in that order as often as possible. The rhythm of the entire performance is as important to establish as is the rhythm of the individual parts. The audience must not be kept waiting between numbers. If a pause is justified by an important scenery change, give the audience an intermission with house lights and a chance to stretch their legs and chat with friends. Try not to overdo this; too many intermissions become a bore!

The length of the program depends somewhat on the calibre of the performers, but remember Doris Humphrey's advice that all dances are too long,[6] and add to that the thought that all dance performances are too long. It is far better to end the performance with the audience on its feet clammering for more than to perform three more pieces to yawning, fidgeting spectators. Remember that the actual minutes of choreography are

[6]Doris Humphrey, *The Art of Making Dances*, ed. Barbara Pollack (New York and Toronto: Rinehart & Co., 1959), p. 159.

doubled at performance time, allowing for exits and en-trances, curtains, and, we hope, applause.

It is better not to send the program to the printer until just before the deadline. The longer you can wait, the less likely are the inevitable changes that must be made for Betsy's skiing accident and John's last-minute decision to transfer to State U. If changes must in fact be made, a printed insert which simply states that Martha Green will dance in place of Barbara Brown in "The Three Strangers" will suffice. If there is not time for that, an announcement can be made prior to the beginning of the performance. It is best not to break the flow of the program with interruptions once it has begun.

When the program has been designed, printed, and distributed, remember that the audience needs house lights now and then in order to read it!

PUBLICITY

Dance, as a means of communication, must be presented to an audience in order for its mission to be accomplished. Choreographers and dancers know when a piece is ready to be presented, and they are usually eager for it to be seen. An audience must be summoned. There are many vehicles for the communication of this readiness to a potential audience. Word of mouth, telephone calls, letters, radio, television and newspaper announcements, posters, photographs, and news releases will help to spread the word. Reputation is also important. If a group has performed previously, those who have seen it will advise others as to whether or not it is worth the investment of time, money, and effort. Families and friends of the dancers can always be counted on, provided that the information is distributed early enough so that the time can be reserved. Reminders at the last minute are also essential.

If school and local newspaper critics are invited, their reviews following the performance will help to generate interest for the future. In general, the more effort the dancers have made in preparation for a performance, the more time should be spent on publicity. For if a dance is worth being presented, all seats in the auditorium should be filled.

TECHNICIANS

A successful dance performance requires more than interesting choreography, appropriate accompaniment, and skilled dancers. An artistic director responsible for the coordination of all parts of the production is needed. In an educational situation, this is generally a dance instructor who is faculty adviser to the dance group. The director is often assisted by a student who is the president or chairperson of the dance group. In addition, there must be sound and lighting technicians, scenery and prop people, stage managers, ushers, curtain pullers, costumers, makeup experts, ticket sellers, and publicity people. Students interested in dance but not quite ready for performance are the most likely candidates for these essential jobs.

The artistic director is responsible for the training of all technicians and for coordinating the technical aspects of the performance with the work of the choreographers and dancers.

The sound and lighting technicians must be knowledgeable in their own areas. However, a good audio technician is not necessarily experienced in dance performance. These specialists must be trained for the particular needs of dancers. Once trained, it is helpful if they can be induced to work with the dance group more than one year. Since most students graduate after four years, an effort should be made to have some apprentices in the wings.

The stage manager controls the actions of dancers and technicians once the performance begins. Therefore, there must be an earphone or walkie-talkie link between them. Stage manager is one of the most critical positions and therefore must be held by a mature individual who can demand and receive complete respect from dancers and technicians. Unfortunately, many artistic directors are forced to assume that role and hence cannot be out front, where they should be, during the performance.

Once chosen and trained, all technicians must agree to be at technical and dress rehearsals as well as at all performances. Last-minute personnel changes are likely to bring about disastrous results. When choreographers and dancers have worked all year on a dance, they deserve the security of knowing that the correct music will be played, the curtain will not close too soon, and the stage will not be blacked out before that final pose!

The dance has been choreographed, reworked a hundred times, and finally taught to the dancers. Now that they know it, it is time to start dancing! Although this statement sounds silly, it cannot be emphasized too strongly that the difference between marking a dance and dancing full-out will determine the success or failure of the presentation. Experienced dancers have mastered the skill of projecting to an audience. If a dancer has mastered his or her craft, is well rehearsed, and is highly motivated to communicate to the audience, projection occurs. Unless the audience is reached, the dancer or choreographer has failed.

In general, the more rehearsals, the better the performance. However, depending on the situation, this is not always practical. If the dancers are full-time students or employees and part-time dancers, rehearsal time can be a problem. The task of finding rehearsal time is not nearly as difficult for solos and duets as it is for group pieces. Everyone knows that a dance choreographed for ten is confusing and disruptive to rehearse when only seven are present, and when a different seven are at the next rehearsal!

The number of rehearsals is not the only factor; the quality of the rehearsal is also important. Videotape is a marvelous device for demonstrating to dancers their technical flaws and the need of more work. It is difficult to convince Susie that she frequently brushes her hair back from her eyes while dancing until she sees it for herself. Videotape can politely but emphatically point out to a group member that his or her timing is just a bit off from the rest of the group. It is wise to arrange for videotaping early enough so that changes or corrections can be made.

Full cast attendance is a must at the dress rehearsal. In addition to all the dancers, this includes the stage manager, lighting crew, sound technicians, curtain pullers, and all the other people who will be involved on opening night. It seems obvious to state that a dress rehearsal requires full dress and makeup, but it is so difficult to achieve! The dress rehearsal must be an exact replica of what is desired for the performance, if the performance is to go as planned. Wrinkled skirts, headgear that falls off, colors of costumes that fade in the chosen light scheme are only a few details that are better discovered before curtain time. There should be no interruptions, so that the performance can be timed. The artistic director can make notes while the rehearsal is proceeding for later discussion with the cast. One last run-through just before the performance often does wonders to release adrenalin and help calm jittery nerves. And performers are apt to dance better on the second run-through.

When student groups are performing, it is sometimes wise to schedule that final rehearsal in the late afternoon of the day of opening night and then serve a light snack on stage while hair is being curled and costumes restitched and the sound tape spliced. It eliminates the worry of wondering whether everyone will arrive in time to warm up and be made up at a reasonably leisurely pace.

Immediately prior to the opening of the curtain, a pep talk is in order. Not only must dancers be checked for such mundane details as runs in tights, forgotten costume effects, and the removal of jewelry and gum, but it is important that they be reminded that if one should fall, start or stop a movement too soon, turn in the wrong direction, or any of the hundreds of other errors that can occur, the audience must be spared that fact. Hide your embarrassment and carry off your mistake with aplomb; who will know the difference?

Professional behavior backstage demands silence, quick costume changes, and the ability to avoid releasing tensions and excitement until after the program is over.

THE CURTAIN CALL

Neophytes to performance often neglect the preparation of a bow or curtain call until the dance has been performed and the audience is on its feet applauding. A soloist can often cover up this oversight by smiling, bowing, and running gracefully to the safety of the wings. If more than one dancer is involved, however, advance planning is essential. What a shame it is when the last impression given to the audience is not on the same highly polished level as the rest of the performance. Depending on the physical situation in which you are performing and on the continuity you want to establish, dancers may take their bows after each dance or may wait until the end, when the entire company is brought forth in an orderly and artistic formation to present a synchronous bow. Sometimes both are done. The bow must be choreographed in the same mood as the dance it follows. The spell created by a beautiful, ethereal character must not be broken when she steps forth to show her classmates that she is in reality the human being in the fourth row of chemistry lab!

Be sure the technicians in the control room are also prepared so that curtains will be opened and closed and lights will be turned on and off at the desired moments. Let's not leave dancers in total darkness groping for that elusive opening in the curtain!

AFTERMATH   When the final curtain comes down and the happy but exhausted dancers run to the dressing room to receive enthusiastic fans bearing flowers and compliments, this is not the end of the performance. Still remaining are the mundane tasks of cleaning up the theatre, returning borrowed costumes and props, and thanking all the people who contributed time and talent. But do not forget the most important ingredient: the choreography. After a performance is the best time to evaluate the dances. Did they succeed in communicating to the audience? It is sometimes possible to gain an inkling of this through newspaper reviews and audience comments. Another way is to listen to the comments of the dancers who performed and those of the dance instructors who watched. In addition to outside sources, the choreographer must evaluate his or her own dance. Changes may need to be made, parts cut or reformed, or a new ending constructed. A willingness to learn, change, reshape, cut, re-create will enable the choreographer to grow.

You will derive much personal satisfaction from taking classes, from learning and performing the dances of others, and from creating original compositions. In addition to becoming a more skilled dancer and a more vibrant person, you will become a more discerning audience for dance performances. Once you have sampled the rewards of dance study, you will no doubt want to continue. You will be eager to learn more about dance by reading and watching dance performances and films.

The appendixes which follow suggest sources for further study.

7

APPENDIXES

APPENDIX A
BIBLIOGRAPHY

History

The following sources, with a few exceptions, were selected because of their coverage of the history of modern dance.

ANDERSON, JACK, *Dance*. New York: Newsweek Books, 1974.

ARMITAGE, MERLE, *Dance Memoranda*. New York: Duell, Sloan & Pearce, 1946.

BANES, SALLY, *Terpsichore in Sneakers: Post-Modern Dance*. Boston: Houghton Mifflin Company, 1979.

BROWN, JEAN MORRISON, ed., *The Vision of Modern Dance*. Princeton, NJ: Princeton Book Company, Publishers, 1979.

COHEN, SELMA JEAN, ed., *Dance As A Theatre Art: Source Readings in Dance History from 1581 to the Present*. New York: Dodd, Mead & Company, 1974.

DE MILLE, AGNES, *The Book of the Dance*. New York: Golden Press, 1963.

HIGHWATER, JAMAKE, *Dance: Rituals of Experience*. New York: A & W Publishers, Inc., 1978.

KENDALL, ELIZABETH, *Where She Danced*. New York: Alfred A. Knopf, Inc., 1979.

KIRSTEIN, LINCOLN, *Dance: A Short History of Classic Theatrical Dancing*. Brooklyn, NY: a Dance Horizons replication, 1969.

KRAUS, RICHARD, and SARAH CHAPMAN, *History of the Dance in Art and Education*, 2nd ed. Englewood Cliffs, NJ: Prentice-Hall, Inc., 1981.

LAWLER, LILLIAN B. *The Dance in Ancient Greece*. Middletown, CT: Weslyan University Press, 1965.

LLOYD, MARGARET, *The Borzoi Book of Modern Dance*. Brooklyn, NY: Dance Horizons, 1970. (reprint)

MAGRIEL, PAUL, *Chronicles of the American Dance: From the Shakers to Martha Graham*. New York: Henry Holt & Co.. 1948. (also paperback, New York: Da Capo, 1978)

Martin, John, *America Dancing: The Background and Person-alities of the Modern Dance*. Brooklyn, NY: Dance Horizons, 1968. (reprint)

—— *The Modern Dance*. New York: Dance Horizons, 1965. (reprint)

Maynard, Olga, *American Modern Dancers: The Pioneers*. New York: Atlantic Monthly Press Book; Boston and Toronto: Little, Brown & Company, 1965.

Mazo, Joseph H., *Prime Movers: The Makers of Modern Dance in America*. New York: William Morrow & Company, Inc., 1977.

McDonagh, Don, *The Rise and Fall and Rise of Modern Dance*. New York: Outerbridge & Dienstfrey, distributed by E.P. Dutton, 1970.

Percival, John, *Experimental Dance*. New York: Universe Books, 1971.

Sachs, Curt, *World History of the Dance*. New York: W.W. Norton & Co., Inc., 1937.

Sorell, Walter, *Dance in Its Time*. Garden City, New York: Anchor Press, Doubleday, 1981.

Terry, Walter, *The Dance in America*. New York: Harper & Brothers Publishers, 1956.

Dancers   Included are autobiographies and biographies of some of the major contributors to the development of modern dance.

Armitage, Merle, ed., *Martha Graham*. Brooklyn, NY: Dance Horizons, 1966. (replication)

Cohen, Selma Jeanne, ed., *Doris Humphrey: An Artist First*. Middletown, CT: Wesleyan University Press, 1972.

Duncan, Isadora, *My Life*. New York: Boni and Liveright, 1927.

Fuller, Loie, *Fifteen Years of a Dancer's Life: With Some Account of Her Distinguished Friends*. New York: Dance Horizons, 1978. (reprint)

Hodgson, Moira, and Thomas Victor, *Quintet: Five American Dance Companies*. New York: William Morrow & Co., Inc., 1976.

Magriel, Paul, ed., *Isadora Duncan*. New York: Henry Holt & Co., 1947.

Sorell, Walter, *Hanya Holm: The Biography of an Artist*. Middletown, CT: Wesleyan University Press, 1969.

Sorell, Walter, ed. & trans., *The Mary Wigman Book*. Middletown, CT: Wesleyan University Press, 1973.

SHAWN, TED, and GRAY POOLE, *One Thousand and One Night Stands*. Garden City, NY: Doubleday & Co., Inc., 1960.

SHELTON, SUZANNE, *Divine Dancer: A Biography of Ruth St. Denis*. Garden City, NY: Doubleday & Co., Inc., 1981.

ST. DENIS, RUTH, *An Unfinished Life*. Brooklyn, NY: a Dance Horizons replication, 1969.

STODELLE, ERNESTINE, *The First Frontier: The Story of Louis Horst and the American Dance*. Cheshire CT: Ernestine Stodelle, 1964.

TERRY, WALTER, *Frontiers of Dance: The Life of Martha Graham*. New York: Thomas Y. Crowell Company, Inc., 1975.

——— *Isadora Duncan: Her Life, Her Art, Her Legacy*. New York: Dodd, Mead & Company, 1964.

———, *Miss Ruth: The "More Living Life" of Ruth St. Denis*. New York: Dodd, Mead & Company, 1969.

———, *Ted Shawn: Father of American Dance*. New York: The Dial Press, 1976.

Theory and Technique

The following sources include the theory and technique of modern dance. A small selected group of ballet books are also included.

CHENEY, GAY, and JANET STRADER, *Modern Dance*, 2nd ed. Boston: Allyn & Bacon, Inc., 1975.

FREED, MARGARET DE HAAN, *A Time to Teach, A Time to Dance*. Sacramento: Jalmar Press, Inc., 1976.

GATES, ALICE, *A New Look at Movement: A Dancer's View*. Minneapolis: Burgess Publishing Co., 1968.

GUILLOT, GENEVIEVE, AND GERMAINE PRUDHOMMEAU, *The Book of Ballet*, trans. Katherine Carson. Englewood Cliffs, NJ: Prentice-Hall, Inc., 1976.

HAMMOND, SANDRA NOLL, *Ballet Basics*. Palo Alto, CA: National Press Books, 1974.

HAWKINS, ALMA M., *Modern Dance in Higher Education*. New York: Bureau of Publications, Teachers College, Columbia University, 1954.

HAYES, ELIZABETH R., *An Introduction to the Teaching of Dance*. New York: The Ronald Press Company, 1964.

HAYS, JOAN F., *Modern Dance*. St. Louis, Toronto, and London: The C.V. Mosby Company, 1981.

H'DOUBLER, MARGARET N., *Dance: A Creative Art Experience*. Madison, WI: University of Wisconsin Press, 1966. (reprint)

HYPES, JEANETTE, ed., *Discover Dance*. Washington: American Alliance for Health, Physical Education and Recreation., 1978.

Jones, Ruth Whitney, and Margaret DeHaan, *Modern Dance in Education: Techniques and Dances.* New York: Bureau of Publications, Teachers College, Columbia University, 1947.

Kirstein, Lincoln; Muriel Stuart; and Carlus Dyer, *The Classic Ballet: Basic Technique and Terminology.* New York: Alfred A. Knopf, Inc., 1977.

Laban, Rudolf von, *Modern Educational Dance*, 2nd ed., rev. Lisa Ullmann, New York and Washington: Frederick A. Praeger, 1968.

Lockhardt, Aileene, and Esther E. Pease, *Modern Dance: Building and Teaching Lessons.* 5th ed. Dubuque, IA: William C. Brown Co., Publishers, 1978.

Martin, John, *Introduction to the Dance.* New York: W.W. Norton & Co., Inc., 1939.

Norris, Dorothy E. Koch, and Reva P. Shiner, *Keynotes to Modern Dance*, 3rd ed. Minneapolis: Burgess Publishing Co., 1969.

Pease, Esther E., *Modern Dance*, 2nd ed. Dubuque, IA: William C. Brown Co., Publishers, 1976.

Penrod, James, and Janice Gudde Plastino, *The Dancer Prepares: Modern Dance for Beginners*, 2nd ed. Palo Alto, CA: Mayfield Publishing Co., 1980.

Poll, Toni, L., *Complete Handbook of Secondary School Dance Activities.* Englewood Cliffs, NJ: Prentice-Hall, Inc., 1977.

Preston, Valerie, *A Handbook for Modern Educational Dance.* London: MacDonald & Evans Ltd., 1963.

Radir, Ruth Anderson, *Modern Dance: For the Youth of America.* New York: A.S. Barnes & Company, Inc., 1944.

Russell, Joan, *Modern Dance in Education.* New York: Frederick A. Praeger, 1968.

Schurman, Nona, and Sharon Leigh Clark, *Modern Dance Fundamentals.* New York: Macmillan, Inc., 1972.

Sherbon, Elizabeth, *On the Count of One: Modern Dance Methods*, 3rd ed. Palo Alto, CA: Mayfield Publishing Co., 1982.

Shurr, Gertrude, and Rachael Dunaven Yocom, *Modern Dance: Techniques and Teaching.* New York: The Ronald Press Company, 1949. (also Dance Horizons reprint, 1980)

Stodelle, Ernestine, *The Dance Technique of Doris Humphrey.* Princeton, NJ: Princeton Book Company, Publishers, 1978.

Turner, Margery J., *Modern Dance for High School and College.* Englewood Cliffs, NJ: Prentice-Hall, Inc., 1960.

Choreography Following are some sources which discuss the theory of the art of choreography. Others are accounts of personal methods of choreography by outstanding choreographers.

COHEN, SELMA JEANNE, *The Modern Dance: Seven Statements of Belief.* Middletown, CT: Wesleyan University Press, 1966.

CUNNINGHAM, MERCE, *Changes: Notes on Choreography,* ed. Frances Starr. New York: Something Else Press, 1968.

ELLFELDT, LOIS, *A Primer for Choreographers.* Palo Alto, CA: National Press Books, 1967.

GRAHAM, MARTHA, *The Notebooks of Martha Graham,* ed. George Platt Lynes, New York: Harcourt Brace Jovanovich, Inc., 1973.

GRAY, MIRIAN, ed., *Focus on Dance V: Composition.* Washington: American Association for Health, Physical Education and Recreation, 1969.

HAWKINS, ALMA M., *Creating Through Dance.* Englewood Cliffs, NJ: Prentice-Hall, Inc., 1964.

HAYES, ELIZABETH R., *Dance Composition and Production: For High Schools and Colleges.* Brooklyn, NY: Dance Horizons, 1981. (reprint)

HORST, LOUIS, *Pre-Classic Dance Forms.* Brooklyn, NY: Dance Horizons, 1968. (reprint)

HORST, LOUIS, and CARROLL RUSSELL, *Modern Dance Forms: In Relation to the Other Modern Arts.* San Francisco: Impulse Publications, 1961. (also Dance Horizons reprint, 1967)

HUGHES, RUSSELL MERIWEATHER, *Dance Composition: The Basic Elements.* Lee, MA: Jacob's Pillow Dance Festival, Inc., 1965.

HUMPHREY, DORIS, *The Art of Making Dances,* ed. Barbara Pollack. New York and Toronto: Rinehart & Co., Inc., 1959; (New York: Grove Press, 1962.)

LOUIS, MURRAY, *Inside Dance.* New York: St. Martin's Press, 1980.

SMITH, JACQUELINE, *Dance Composition: A Practical Guide for Teachers.* Surrey: Lepus Books, Henry Kimpton Ltd., 1976.

TURNER, MARGERY J., with RUTH GRAUERT and ARLENE ZALLMAN, *New Dance: Approaches to Nonliteral Choreography.* Pittsburgh: University of Pittsburgh Press, 1971. (paperback reissue 1976)

Performance The following texts offer helpful suggestions for those involved with the various aspects of dance performance.

A Guide to Dance Production: "On With the Show." Reston, VA: National Dance Association of the American Alliance for Health, Physical Education, Recreation and Dance, 1981.

BASCOM, FRANCES, and CHARLOTTE IREY, *Costume Cues.* Washington: American Association for Health, Physical Education, and Recreation, 1952.

CORSON, RICHARD, *Stage Makeup,* 5th ed. Englewood Cliffs, NJ: Prentice-Hall, Inc., 1975.

ELLFELDT, LOUIS, and EDWIN CARNES, *Dance Production Handbook; or, Later Is Too Late.* Palo Alto, CA: National Press Books, 1971.

GILBERT, PIA, and AILEENE LOCKHART, *Music for the Modern Dance.* Dubuque, IA: William C. Brown Co., Publishers, 1961.

LIPPINCOTT, GERTRUDE, ed., *Dance Production.* Washington: American Association for Health, Physical Education and Recreation, 1956, 1960.

MELCER, FANNIE H., *Staging the Dance.* Dubuque, IA: William C. Brown Co., Publishers, 1955.

PARKER, W. OREN, and HARVEY K. SMITH, *Scene Design and Stage Lighting,* 3rd ed. New York: Holt, Rinehart & Winston, 1974.

SCHLAICH, JOAN, and BETTY DuPONT, *Dance: The Art of Production.* St. Louis: The C.V. Mosby Company, 1977.

SELDEN, SAMUEL, and HUNTON D. SELLMAN, *Stage Scenery and Lighting,* 3rd ed. New York: Appleton-Century-Crofts, 1959.

WARFEL, WILLIAM, B., *Handbook of Stage Lighting Graphics,* 2nd ed. New York: Drama Book Specialists, 1974.

Anatomy, Health, and Injuries

This group of books includes essential information for any dancer.

ARNHEIM, DANIEL D., *Dance Injuries: Their Prevention and Care,* 2nd ed. St. Louis: The C.V. Mosby Company, 1980.

FEATHERSTONE, DONALD F., in collaboration with Rona Allen, *Dancing Without Danger,* 2nd ed. South Brunswick, NJ, and New York: A.S. Barnes & Company, Inc., 1977.

SWEIGARD, LULU, *Human Movement Potential: Its Ideokinetic Facilitation.* New York: Dodd, Mead & Co., 1974.

VINCENT, L.M., *Competing With the Sylph.* Mission, KS: Andrews and McMeel, Inc., 1979.

————, *The Dancer's Book of Health.* Kansas City, KS: Sheed, Andrews and McMeel, 1978.

Reference The following are general reference books and others with emphasis on practical information.

CHUJOY, ANATOLE, and P.W. MANCHESTER, *The Dance Encyclopedia*. New York: Simon & Schuster, Inc., 1967.

CLARKE, MARY, and DAVID VAUGHAN, EDS., *The Encyclopedia of Dance and Ballet*. New York: G.P. Putnam's Sons, 1977.

JACOB, ELLEN, and CHRISTOPHER JONAS, *Dance in New York*. New York: Quick-Fox, 1980.

LOREN, TERI, *The Dancer's Companion*. New York: The Dial Press, 1978.

LOVE, PAUL, *Modern Dance Terminology*. New York: Kamin Dance Publishers, 1953.

McDONAGH, DON, *Complete Guide to Modern Dance*. Garden City, NY: Doubleday & Co., Inc., 1976.

RAFFÉ, W.G., *Dictionary of the Dance*. New York: A.S. Barnes & Company, Inc., 1964. (reissued 1975)

REYNOLDS, NANCY, ed., *The Dance Catalogue*. New York: Harmony Books, 1979.

Periodicals Some dance magazines and journals of special interest to modern dancers are listed below.

Ballet News
Published by the Metropolitan Opera Guild, Inc.
1865 Broadway
New York, NY 10023
monthly
(includes modern dance)

Dance Chronicle: Studies in Dance and the Related Arts
Published by Marcel Dekker, Inc.
270 Madison Avenue
New York, NY 10016
quarterly

Dancemagazine
Danad Publishing Company
1180 Avenue of the Americas
New York, NY 10036
monthly

Dance Research Journal
Published by Congress on Research in Dance
Dance Department
Education 675 D
New York University
35 West 4th Street
New York, NY 10003
semi-annual

Dance Scope
Published by the American Dance Guild
570 7th Avenue
New York, NY 10018
quarterly.

Design
Heldref Publications
4000 Albermarle St., N. W.
Suite 500
Washington, DC, 20016

The Drama Review
51 West 4th Street
New York, NY 10012
quarterly
(includes experimental dance)

Focus on Dance
Published by the National Section on Dance;
American Alliance for Health, Physical Education,
Recreation, and Dance
1900 Association Drive
Reston, VA 22091
published every 2 years

Journal of Physical Education, Recreation and Dance
American Alliance for Health, Physical Education,
Recreation, and Dance
1900 Association Drive
Reston, VA 22091
10 issues per year

Performing Arts Journal
325 Spring Street
New York, NY 10013
triannual
(includes dance)

Journals no longer being published but useful to dance scholars are:

Dance Index
Dance Observer
Dance Perspectives
Impulse: The Annual of Contemporary Dance

Book Distributors Selected distributors of dance books are listed here.

*American Alliance for Health, Physical Education,
Recreation, and Dance*
Order from AAHPERD Publications

Dept. V, P.O. Box 870
Lanham, MD 20801
(publications and audiovisuals)

The American Dance Guild Book Club
Suydam Road
RD3
Somerset, NJ 08873
(a dance book club)

The Ballet Shop
1887 Broadway
New York, NY 10023
(dance books and periodicals)

Children's Music Center Inc.
5373 West Pico Boulevard
Los Angeles, CA 90019
(Dancers Shop)
(dance books, records, percussion instruments, and audio equipment)

Da Capo Press, Inc.
227 West 17th Street
New York, NY 10011
(dance books)

Dance Horizons, Inc.
1801 East 26th Street
Brooklyn, NY 11229
(publisher of dance books)

The Dance Mart
P.O. Box 48, Homecrest Station
Brooklyn, NY 11229
(distributor of dance books)

Footnotes
F. Randolph Associates, Inc.
P.O. Box 328 (1300 Arch Street)
Philadelphia, PA 19105
(dance books, records, audiovisuals, and accessories)

Libraries Most large city and university libraries own good collections of dance literature but the most complete collection of dance books, periodicals, films, clippings, photographs and memorabilia is housed at

The Dance Collection
The Library and Museum of the
Performing Arts at Lincoln Center

111 Amsterdam Avenue (at 64th Street)
New York, NY 10023
Genevieve Oswald, curator

APPENDIX B
Music Composers

This is not a comprehensive list of composers who have written music for dance; instead it is a suggested list of composers of appropriate music for dance composition.

Anderson, Leroy
Babbitt, Milton
Bach, Johann Sebastian
Badings, Henk
Barber, Samuel
Bartók, Béla
Beethoven, Ludwig von
Berg, Alban
Bernstein, Leonard
Bolling, Claude
Brahms, Johannes
Britten, Benjamin
Brubeck, Dave
Cage, John
Carlos, Walter
Chavez, Carlos
Chopin, Frédéric
Copland, Aaron
Cowell, Henry
Czerny, Carl
Debussy, Claude
de Falla, Emanuel
Dello Joio, Norman
Dukas, Paul
Ellington, Duke
Foss, Lucas
George, Earl
Gershwin, George
Goodman, Benny
Gould, Morton
Grainger, Percy
Grieg, Edvard
Handel, George Frederick
Haydn, Franz Josef

Hindemith, Paul
Horst, Louis
Ives, Charles
Joplin, Scott
Kenton, Stan
Lewis, Ramsey
Lloyd, Norman
Lobos, Villa
Mancini, Henry
Mangione, Chuck
Mendelssohn, Felix
Mozart, Wolfgang Amadeus
Ponty, Jean-Luc
Prokofiev, Sergei
Rachmaninov, Sergei
Randall, J.K.
Ravel, Maurice
Riegger, Wallingford
Saint-Saëns, Charles Camille
Satie, Erik
Schoenberg, Arnold
Schubert, Franz
Schuman, William
Schumann, Robert
Sessions, Roger
Shostakovich, Dmitri
Stravinsky, Igor
Tchaikovsky, Peter
Thompson, Virgil
Varèse, Edgard
Vivaldi, Antonio
Webern, Anton
Williams, Ralph Vaughn

Records This list of records includes mainly those which contain music written specifically for modern dance classes. A few selected recordings are included because of their usefulness as accompaniment for improvisation.

Ballet Barre for Modern Dancers
Composed and performed by Rosanne Soifer
Directed by Alice Teirstein
D 707 Footnotes

Composition for Synthesizer
Arel, Davidovsky, El Dabh, Luening, Ussachevsky
Columbia-Princeton Electronics
Center MS 6566

The Dancer Creates
By John Colman
Directed by Joan McCaffrey
DRLP 3086

Drums, Drums, and More Drums
EDLP 10002

Electronic Music
Phillips Stereo # PHS 600-047

First Primer of Modern Dance
By Steffi Nossen
Music by Jess Meeker
SLP 1004

For Contemporary Dance
By Hanya Holm
DRLP 3046

Four Swinging Seasons
By the Gunter Noris Trio
Capitol International
Stereo # SP-10547

Freda D. Miller, Music for Dance
1. *Accompaniment for Dance Technique*
2. *Second Album for Dance*
3. *Third Album for Dance*
4. *Music for Rhythms and Dance*
5. *Fifth Album for Dance*

Improvisations for Modern Dance
Volumes I and II
By Sarah Malament

Keynotes to Modern Dance
Music by Cola Heiden
Book by Dorothy E. Koch Norris and Reva Shiner
610-*Fundamental and Intermediate*
Locomotor Movements

611-*Traditional Forms: Musical Forms-
Pre-Classic Suite*
612-*Advanced Development of Rhythm-
Suggested Compositions*

*Kinetic Transparencies:
Music for Modern Dance*
Composed and performed by Gwendolyn Watson
OLP 121

Library of Music for Dance
by Ruth White
cc 609 *Fundamentals of Music*
cc 610 *Motivations for Modern Dance*
cc 611 *Motifs for Dance Composition*
cc 612 *Music for Contemporary Dance*, vol. 1
cc 613 *Music for Contemporary Dance*, vol. 2

Modern Dance
Created for Gus Giordano
Pianist, Eileen Cohan
Orion

Modern Dance
By Betty Keig and Madeline S. Nixon
502 *Music for Techniques*
503 *Music for Composition*

Modern Dance
Manual by Bruce King
KLP 4010

Modern Dance
By Liz Williams
Music by Elizabeth Smith
DRLP 4002

Modern Dance Technique Environments
Volumes I and II
By Craig Kupka
DRLP 4247

Music for Contemporary Dance
By John Colman
Directed by Oliver Kostock
DRLP 3046

Music for Contemporary Dance
By Norman Walker and Ernest Lubin
SRLP 406

Music for Contemporary Dance Technique
By Carmen DeLavallade and Edward Muller
elementary and intermediate
DRLP 4039 and 4040

Music for Modern Dance
By Mary Anthony and Cameron McCosh
DRLP 3053

Music for Modern Dance
Directed by Marilyn V. Patton
Composed by Anthony Crescione
DRLP 4193

Music for Modern Dance
By Deborah Zall and Edward Muller
DRLP 4042

Music for the Modern Dance
By Pia Gilbert
Manual by Aileene Lockhart
DRLP 4015

Music for Modern Dance Technique
By Bertram Ross and Edward Muller
(3 records)
DRLP 4086, 4087, 4088

Music for Movement No. 1 and No. 2
By Kay Ortmans
KOP-131, KOP-132

Piano Accompaniment for Modern Dance
Volumes 1 and 2
Music by Rosanne Soifer
Directed by Muriel Gordon
SLPS-101, SLPS-102

Rhythms and Textures: Piano Improvisation for Modern Dance
By Edward Muller
Directed by Bertram Ross
DRLP 4139

Sound Patterns: A Documentary of Man-made and Nature Sounds
Scholastics FX 1630

The Sting
Music by Scott Joplin
Adapted by Marvin Hamlisch
MCA Records

Switched-On Bach
By Walter Carlos
Columbia
Stereo #MS-7194

Toccata for Percussion
By Carlos Chavez
Capitol P-8299

Record Companies and Distributors

These are several of the major producers and distributors of records for modern dance class.

Cheviot Corporation
P.O. Box 34485
Los Angeles, CA 90034

Classroom Materials Company
93 Myrtle Drive
Great Neck, NY 11021

Educational Activities, Inc.
P.O. Box 392
Freeport, NY 11520

Educational Record Sales
157 Chalmers Street
New York, NY 10007

Hoctor Dance Records, Inc.
159 Franklyn Turnpike
Waldwick, NJ 07463

Freda Miller Records for Dance
131 Bayview Avenue
Northport, NY 11768

Kimbo Educational
P.O. Box 477
Long Branch, NJ 07740

Sarah Malament
3215 Netherland Avenue
Bronx, NY 10463

Orion Records, Inc.
614 Davis Street
Evanston, IL 60201

Kay Ortmans Productions
11667 Alba Road
Ben Lomond, CA 95005

Rhythms Productions Recordings
13152 Grant Avenue
Downey, CA 90242

S and R Records
1609 Broadway
New York, NY 10017

Scholastic, Inc.
900 Sylvan Avenue
Englewood Cliffs, NJ 07632

Statler Records, Inc.
1795 Express Drive North
Smithtown, NY 11787

Synchronized Sound
P.O. Box 305
Purchase, NY 10577

Sources for the selection, rental, and purchase of films and videotapes which are recommended are listed below.

1. *Directories*

DURKIN, KATHLEEN, and PAUL LEVESQUE, eds. *Catalogue of Dance Films*, compiled by Susan Braun and Dorothy H. Currie. New York: Dance Films Association, Inc., 1974

MUELLER, JOHN, *Dance Film Directory: An Annotated and Evaluative Guide to Films on Ballet and Modern Dance*. Princeton, NJ: Princeton Book Company, Publishers, 1979.

2. *Association*
(publishes a catalogue and a newsletter and sponsors an annual film festival)

Dance Films Association, Inc.
250 West 57th Street
Room 2201
New York, NY 10019

3. *Distributors of audivisuals*
(representative list)

Athletic Institute
Castlewood Drive
North Palm Beach, FL 33408

Blackwood Productions, Inc.
251 West 57th Street
New York, NY 10019

Cinema 16
175 Lexington Avenue
New York, NY 10016

Corinth Films
410 East 62nd Street
New York, NY 10021

Dance Film Archive
University of Rochester
Rochester, NY 14627

Educational Media Services
Brigham Young University
290 HRCB
Provo, UT 84602

Educational Resources
University of South Florida
Tampa, FL 33620

Extension Media Center
University of California
2223 Fulton Street
Berkeley, CA 94720

NET Film Service
Indiana University
Audio-Visual Center
Bloomington, IN 47401

Syracuse University Film Library
Syracuse, NY 13210

Visual Aids Service
University of Illinois
Champaign, IL 61820

4. *To Review Films*

The Dance Collection
The Library and Museum of the
Performing Arts
Lincoln Center
111 Amsterdam Avenue (at 64th Street) New York, NY 10023

APPENDIX D
SUPPLIES
Leotards and
other essentials

The distributors listed below are mainly concerned with
the sale of clothing for dance. Several also furnish books,
records, and other dance accessories.

Baum's Incroporated
106 South 11th Street
Philadelphia, PA 19107

Capezio
1612 Broadway
New York, NY 10019

D.W. Danskin, Inc.
1114 Avenue of the Americas
New York, NY 10036

Footlight Shops of San Francisco
126 Post Street
San Francisco, CA 94108

J.C. Hall Dance Supplies, Inc.
210 Pearl Street
Hartford, CT 06103

Leo's Advance Theatrical Company
2451 North Sacramento
Chicago, IL 60647

Taffy's
701 Beta Drive
Cleveland, OH 44143

For more information about dance supplies consult:

Dancemagazine Annual
(see address under Periodicals)

Simon's Directory of Theatrical
Materials, Services and Information
Published by Package Publicity Service
1564 Broadway
New York, NY 10036

INDEX

Editor's Note: Page numbers in italics indicate illustrations.

List of Dances